ROBERT DE REIMS

ROBERT DE REIMS

Songs and Motets

EDITED, TRANSLATED, AND INTRODUCED BY

EGLAL DOSS-QUINBY
GAËL SAINT-CRICQ
SAMUEL N. ROSENBERG

The Pennsylvania State University Press
University Park, Pennsylvania

Cataloging-in-publication data is on file with the
Library of Congress.

Printed in the United States of America
Published by The Pennsylvania State University Press,
University Park, PA 16802-1003

The Pennsylvania State University Press is a member
of the Association of University Presses.

It is the policy of The Pennsylvania State University
Press to use acid-free paper. Publications on
uncoated stock satisfy the minimum requirements
of American National Standard for Information
Sciences—Permanence of Paper for Printed Library
Material, ANSI Z39.48–1992.

We dedicate this volume to the memory of our colleague
Samuel N. Rosenberg, a great scholar, an even greater friend.

Contents

Acknowledgments

The Old French text and Modern French translation of song no. 9 first appeared in *"Sottes chansons contre Amours": Parodie et burlesque au Moyen Âge*, edited, translated, and introduced by Eglal Doss-Quinby, Marie-Geneviève Grossel, and Samuel N. Rosenberg (Paris: Honoré Champion, 2010, pp. 120–22); a portion of the introduction, regarding what we know about Robert de Reims, is borrowed from the same volume (pp. 16–17), translated into English for use here; republication, with modifications, is done with permission of the publisher and the authors. Preliminary versions of the Old French texts and English translations of songs nos. 4a, 5a, 7a, and 8a were first prepared by Eglal Doss-Quinby and Samuel N. Rosenberg for "Genre, Attribution and Authorship in the Thirteenth Century: Robert de Reims vs 'Robert de Rains,'" by Gaël Saint-Cricq, *Early Music History* 38 (2019): 141–213, appendix IV, pp. 205–10.

We are grateful to Jeffrey S. Ankrom for his advice and kind support in the process of submitting our manuscript for review. We also wish to offer special thanks to our expert reviewers for their most generous attention to our manuscript.

Abbreviations

BIBLIOGRAPHICAL DATA

M   Mass, as catalogued in Ludwig 1910
O   Office, as catalogued in Ludwig 1910
RS   Spanke 1955
vdB   van den Boogaard 1969

MANUSCRIPTS

fol.   folio
r   recto
v   verso
♫   music

MOTETS

perf. perfection

Manuscripts Cited

The manuscripts cited below are those to which reference is made in abbreviated form in the present volume. A complete listing and a bibliography may be found in Linker 1979, 23–69. See also Jeanroy 1918; Spanke 1955; and Aubrey 2001. For sources that preserve polyphonic music, see Ludwig 1910, 1964–78; Gennrich 1957; Reaney 1966; Everist 1989; and Van der Werf 1989.

TROUVÈRE MANUSCRIPTS

A   Arras, Bibliothèque municipale, 657
C   Bern, Burgerbibliothek, 389
F   London, British Library, Egerton 274
H   Modena, Biblioteca estense, R4, 4
I   Oxford, Bodleian Library, Douce 308
K   Paris, Bibliothèque de l'Arsenal, 5198 ("Chansonnier de l'Arsenal")
L   Paris, Bibliothèque nationale de France, fr. 765
M   Paris, Bibliothèque nationale de France, fr. 844 ("Chansonnier du Roi," song corpus)
N   Paris, Bibliothèque nationale de France, fr. 845
O   Paris, Bibliothèque nationale de France, fr. 846 ("Chansonnier Cangé")
P   Paris, Bibliothèque nationale de France, fr. 847
R   Paris, Bibliothèque nationale de France, fr. 1591
T   Paris, Bibliothèque nationale de France, fr. 12615 ("Chansonnier de Noailles," song corpus)
U   Paris, Bibliothèque nationale de France, fr. 20050 ("Chansonnier de Saint-Germain-des-Prés")
V   Paris, Bibliothèque nationale de France, fr. 24406
X   Paris, Bibliothèque nationale de France, n. a. fr. 1050 ("Chansonnier Clairambault")
Z   Siena, Biblioteca comunale degli Intronati, H. X. 36
a   Rome, Biblioteca Apostolica Vaticana, Reg. lat. 1490

Cl   Paris, Bibliothèque nationale de France, n. a. fr. 13521 ("La Clayette")

F   Florence, Biblioteca Medicea Laurenziana, Pluteus 29, 1

Mo   Montpellier, Bibliothèque interuniversitaire, Section Médecine, H 196

MüA   Munich, Bayerische Staatsbibliothek, gallo-rom. 42 and Berlin, Staatsbibliothek zu Berlin, Musikabteilung 55 MS 14 (Johannes Wolf fragments)

N   Paris, Bibliothèque nationale de France, fr. 12615 ("Chansonnier de Noailles," motet corpus)

R   Paris, Bibliothèque nationale de France, fr. 844 ("Chansonnier du Roi," motet corpus)

W₂   Wolfenbüttel, Herzog August Bibliothek, Helmstedt 1099 (Heinemann 1206)

Tables

Introduction

Robert de Reims, also known as "La Chievre de Rains," was a poet-composer from Champagne, in the northeast of France, active sometime between 1190 and 1220. He appears to have been influential in the literary circles of Arras, in the region of Artois. Little else is known about Robert, beyond the fact that he was among the earliest trouvères. Thirteen compositions set to music may be attributed to him: nine songs (*chansons*) and four polyphonic motets.[1] Despite their quite limited number, these pieces show broad distribution in thirteenth-century sources, with as many as forty-seven occurrences—thirty-six as chansons preserved in songbooks and eleven as polyphonic compositions in liturgical books or motet collections. Such distribution, moreover, persists through the thirteenth century and beyond, from the oldest stratum of the Chansonnier de Saint-Germain-des-Prés (manuscript *U*), copied in the early 1220s, to manuscripts *a*, *O*, and *R*, produced at the beginning of the fourteenth century. A critical edition of Robert's songs was last published in German in 1899 by Wilhelm Mann. This edition does not present the motets; it does not include translations from the Old French or, more significantly, the music transmitted in the medieval sources. The present volume fills this gap and takes a fresh look at the work of this neglected trouvère.

The corpus of Robert de Reims is exceptional on a number of fronts. First, Robert composed both conventional and farcical love songs. He is the earliest trouvère known to have composed a *sotte chanson contre Amours* (or "silly song against Love"), a lyric countertext whose parodic-comedic features allow for the simultaneous subversion and celebration of the traditional courtly love song. His participation in this playful mode pushes back the accepted origins of the genre by several decades.[2]

Robert's corpus also poses the intriguing question of trouvère participation in the development of the polyphonic repertory. His work was clearly at the nexus of monophonic song and polyphony, with no fewer than four of his nine songs also appearing as upper parts of polyphonic motets elsewhere and two of them, moreover, transcribed as clausulæ in liturgical sources. Robert's production thus allows us to discover the role of a recognized trouvère in the interplay of composition and recomposition of works through their various monophonic and polyphonic recastings. Critically, it reveals not only that some trouvères took part in the development of polyphony but also that their involvement occurred very early in the history of the motet, even influencing the enrichment of liturgical corpora. The case of Robert de Reims jostles and tempers the standard history of the chanson and motet, and it also contributes to filling in the blanks in our knowledge of the compositional and cultural background of these genres.

Robert de Reims was a master of not only conjoining two historically different treatments of vocal music—monophonic and polyphonic—but also writing verse for such settings. Robert was practiced at the art of versification: he lavished particular care on the phonic harmony of his words. Acoustic luxuriance and expertise in rhyming, grounded in the play of echoes and variations, constitute the stylistic hallmark of his poetry: rhymes of the sort called rich, leonine, derived, paronymic, equivocal, annexed, or echoing abound in his poetry, along with other sound patterns, such as alliteration. Indeed, the first specimens of intensive echo rhyming are found in Robert's lyrics, and the quality of his echoed rhymes has long been highlighted by literary historians. His poetic skill is a convincing companion to his musical artistry.

Robert de Reims, dit La Chievre: What We Know, What We Can Surmise

As his name indicates, Robert de Reims, surnamed "La Chievre,"[3] came from the cathedral city of Reims. His dates are not certain; there continues to be scholarly debate surrounding Robert's presumed relations with his southern counterparts, the troubadours, and the probable dating of the manuscript sources of his compositions.

Whereas his first editor, Wilhelm Mann (1898), situated the trouvère's career at the end of the twelfth century, the French philologist Alfred Jeanroy (1899) argued for the middle or even the end of the thirteenth, particularly citing the poet's language and the versification of his songs. According to Madeleine Tyssens, the witness of the Chansonnier de Saint-Germain-des-Prés strongly suggests assigning Robert's corpus no earlier a date than the end of the thirteenth century, due to the fact that the first part of the collection—a repertory comprising the great classics of the late twelfth century and poets associated with the first half of the thirteenth, as well as later figures, such as Colin Muset—cannot be earlier than 1240 (Tyssens 1991, 391, 396; Tyssens 2015, xix–xx). Aurelio Roncaglia has countered that Robert's songs include "toute une série de dérivations directes, et très proches, de Marcabru" (a whole series of direct, and very close, derivations from [the troubadour] Marcabru), which would argue in favor of the first half of the thirteenth century rather than the second (Tyssens 1991, 397).

Marie-Geneviève Grossel (1994, 485) situates the literary production of Robert de Reims beginning in 1213, the date of a song to the Virgin by Moniot d'Arras, *De haut liu muet la cançons que je cant* (RS 304), which, as Holger Petersen Dyggve (1938, 60–62, 66) has demonstrated, is a contrafact of Robert de Reims's *Plaindre m'estuet de la bele en chantant* (RS 319, 320; our song no. 2). Moreover, she associates Robert de Reims with Audefroi le Bastart and Conon de Béthune, whom she considers more or less contemporaries.

The evidence of the Chansonnier de Saint-Germain-des-Prés corroborates such dating and might even allow us to place Robert's activity somewhat earlier, although nothing points to before ca. 1190, as Robert Lug has argued.[4] The main section of this manuscript, copied in Metz in 1231 (Lug 2000), constitutes the earliest compilation of troubadour and trouvère songs (*U*, compositions nos. 1 through 177). It includes three chansons by Robert de Reims (nos. 53, 56, 63), all three occurring in the subdivision of this early part that Lug (2012, 470) calls the "Proto-Chansonnier" (nos. 1–91), which he posits was gathered ca. 1223. The second half of the proto-chansonnier (nos. 40–91) offers a collection of "old rarities"—numerous songs not encountered elsewhere, others recorded only in the closely related manuscript *C*, whose composers we know solely by way of attribution in *C*. It is among these "old rarities" that we find Robert's three chansons, works that place their composer among Lug's "pioneers" and "old masters." Lug advances the hypothesis that Robert de Reims was the earliest known "town trouvère," and it appears that he enjoyed a certain popularity, since no fewer than thirty-six manuscript versions of his nine chansons have been preserved. In her recent edition and analysis of manuscript *U*, Tyssens (2015, xx–xxii) remains noncommittal regarding the early date of gathering advocated by Lug.

Grossel (1994, 485) mentions the possibility that our trouvère was in contact with northern courts, "l'inspiration et le ton de Robert de Reims [ayant] peu à voir avec les habitudes des cercles champenois" (the inspiration and tone of Robert de Reims having little in common with the ways of Champenois circles). Lug also supposes that Robert had an influence on the trouvères active in and around the city of Arras (poets who are not represented in the proto-chansonnier; 2012, 457).

The Corpus and Its Manuscript Tradition

Nine songs are attributed to "Robert de Rains" or "La Chievre de Rains," depending on the manuscript. Although small quantitatively, this corpus enjoyed a wide and lasting reception in medieval sources. As detailed in tables 1 and 2, thirty-six occurrences of Robert's nine chansons[5] and eleven occurrences of his four polyphonic compositions (nine as motets, two as clausulæ) are extant. These forty-seven occurrences and their different settings range across the entire spectrum of poetico-musical sources—from

U at the very beginning of the thirteenth century to *a, O*, and *R* at the start of the fourteenth.[6]

The precise attribution of the songs appears variously in trouvère chansonniers as *Robert de rains* for songs nos. 1 (*NPX*), 2 (*N⁷X*), 3 (*KNPX*), 4 (*KNPX*), 5 (*X*), 6 (*X*), 7 (*X*), and 8 (*X*), or as *la (le, li) chievre (chevre, kievre) de rains (reims)* for songs nos. 1 (*K*), 2 (*KP*), 3 (*CMT*), and 9 (*MTU*). Attributions to *Blondelz* for song no. 1 (*C*) and *monnios* for no. 3 (*R*) have been rejected.[8] It would appear that the rubricators of *NPX* favored the name *Robert*, and those of *MTU* favored *la chievre*, whereas the rubricator of *K* used both names interchangeably. Motets and clausulæ are recorded anonymously, as is normal in those repertories.

Gaël Saint-Cricq (2019) has made the case elsewhere that four songs attributed to Robert de Reims (nos. 4a, 5a, 7a, 8a) originated as motets that were later adapted (that is, stripped of their tenor) and augmented with one or more stanzas by an anonymous continuator. From the point of view of their distribution in the manuscript sources, the five "genuine" chansons and four chansons/motets exhibit clearly different treatments. Among Robert's five "genuine" chansons (nos. 1, 2, 3, 6, 9), three (nos. 1, 3, 9) appear in the first stratum of manuscript *U*, which contains the oldest surviving trouvère compositions, stemming from the years 1200–1220. Unlike most other works in *U*, Robert's songs were copied repeatedly throughout the century. Indeed, the three songs copied in *U* were then recopied in *H* in the middle of the century, *F* in the second half, *MT* sometime around 1260–70, and *C* in the last quarter of the thirteenth.[9] On the other hand, there is no trace in these chansonniers of the chansons derived from motets. It is known, however, that these four works already existed, for *Qant voi le douz tens venir* (4b), *L'autrier de jouste un rivage* (5b), and *Main s'est levee Aëlis* (8b) were copied in the 1250s in their motet form in *MüA* and *W₂*,[10] and as early as the 1240s as clausulæ in *F* in the case of the first two. In fact, except for the group *KNPX*, the sources maintain a generic distinction between Robert's chansons and his motets—the former transmitted in songbooks and the latter in polyphonic collections—a separation that was traditional in the transmission of these two musical genres until the end of the thirteenth century.

As Saint-Cricq (2019) has demonstrated, thirteen chansonniers preserve the full set of five chansons, but none, apart from *KNPX*, includes any of the four chansons/motets, whether in the chanson or motet version. It is only in the "mega-compilation" *KNPX*, apparently created from one and the same large anthology in the decades 1270/1280,[11] that the motets are presented in the form of songs. In other words, songs first conceived as motets to which stanzas were added later are peculiar to *KNPX* and the years 1270/1280, and thus considerably past the time of Robert's death. Robert obviously was active in the making of the four chansons/motets, but as the poet-composer of the initial stanzas, that is, of the motet text and, presumably, of the motet music as well. If, as Saint-Cricq has argued, he was not the author of the supplementary stanzas found in the chanson versions (which were penned by an anonymous author hiding behind the attribution "Robert de Rains"), the four chansons/motets appearing in *KNPX* can be viewed as apocryphal, and, with respect to these four works, "the 'real' Robert de Reims is not quite the 'Robert de Rains' of the chansonniers, offering a case where attribution does not exactly match authorship" (Saint-Cricq 2019, 171).

Thematic Content

Eclecticism is the hallmark of this repertory, which displays a variety of themes and lyric genres, ranging from the courtly chanson to its parodic counterblast.

Most of Robert's compositions are in the high register. *Bien s'est Amors honie* (no. 1) is a song of courtly love; it is not, however, a song of hope or satisfaction, but a bitter expression of disappointment in love, a song of recrimination against not a particular belovèd but against Love itself. More than pained resignation, though, the "I" of the piece seeks death, and at the very hands of that traitorous force. Two of the six manuscripts transmitting this chanson turn the cry of disappointment into a statement addressed to the singer's lady, bringing God into view as well. His desire now is no longer for death but for acceptance of his fate as a man both hurt and healed by the vagaries of Love. He ends by acceding to the inevitable, the "sweet martyrdom" of love.

The chanson *Plaindre m'estuet de la bele en chantant* (no. 2) is, likewise, a work in the high register and an expression of courtly love, but in a more positive vein. Opening in a conventional manner, with an invocation of the singer/lover's need to sing, it quickly goes on to lament the challenge of being in love, of desiring satisfaction, of "serving" the belovèd in the hope of reaching that end, and of beseeching the "aid" of the nonpareil lady. It is meant as a heartfelt declaration of love and expectation. Here too, two manuscripts (one the same as and the other different from the two that transmit additional lines in the case of *Bien s'est Amors honie*) record a complementary message. The added stanza steps back from the (relative) specificity of the foregoing in order to offer a rather generalizing view of the uplifting, indeed ennobling, effect that true love can have on a man's heart.

The theme of *Qui bien veut Amors descrivre* (no. 3) is very much in keeping with the thrust of the preceding pieces, though the courtly message in this case is centered on Love itself. Moreover, the form of the chanson is decidedly different, as Robert seems here to be making his way through a set of variations on the subject of Love. Each stanza offers an elaboration of the seemingly contradictory characteristics and effects of Love: it is good and bad; it brings pleasure and pain; it is generous and miserly; it is ruled by chance and is unpredictable . . . In the end, La Chievre, the composer-singer himself, takes credit for this litany of descriptive features, presented as an artist's generic portrayal of Love, without regard for any particular lover or lover's experience. Three stanzas incorporate the formulaic "Love is . . . ," and every stanza is punctuated by a refrain, a distich that remains unaltered through the five stanzas of the text and thus serves, in its cyclicity, to underscore the notion of theme and variations. Four of the numerous manuscript sources of this chanson record an additional stanza, interpolated between stanza 4 and Robert's summation and declaration of authorship. Even in view of the not-uncommon fluidity of chanson transmission, this patched piece of bromidic counsel looks ill-suited to its alleged context.

Again in the rather staid poetic world of the chanson, *Quant fueillissent li buison* (no. 7a) is sung by a nameless courtly figure, an "I," a poet-composer subject to the will of Love. At the same time, the setting is that of spring, verdant renewal, and amorous expectancy; it is nature, obliging the minstrel to follow the example of the birds and sing. As the song's two different refrains make clear, the season, although consonant with uplift and brightness, also offers a bleak prospect of failure. The vernal setting suggests both possibilities—one through imitation, the other through contrast.

Quite different in spirit is *Quant voi le douz tens venir* (no. 4a), which celebrates the joyful efflorescence of spring and at the same time laments the newly loveless plight of the "I" of the poem. The text expresses an adoring description of the maiden whom the speaker yearns to win (back)—a description readily conflated with the vernal appeal of the song's natural setting. The seasonal imbrication of the piece is underlined by its free, somewhat irregular, yet intricate rhythm, expressed not only in its patterns of rhyming but also in the occurrence of dancelike exogenous refrains that change from stanza to stanza.

Robert's eclectic series of compositions includes the pastourelle *L'autrier de jouste un rivage* (no. 5a), whose love-object in this case is, again, a desirable maiden, though hardly of a courtly caste and portrayed not as a mute figure but as a speaking participant in a miniature play. What begins as a springtime narrative quickly evolves into dialogue and the shepherdess's rejection of the narrator and his proffered suit in favor of her faithful off-stage Robin. Typical of the genre is the text's inclusion of a reference to music and at least one exogenous refrain; see our Commentary.

Touse de vile champestre (no. 6) is another pastourelle, where, even more than in *L'autrier de jouste un rivage*, we find a liltingly musical scene; here, both the shepherdess and her shepherd-mate Robin are on stage and speaking, with no interloper in sight. They sing and they dance; they satisfy their appetite for food and drink as they do for each other. This is unadulterated rustic pleasure, quite different from the experience recounted in the first pastourelle—which nicely serves it as a perhaps intended prelude.

The composition *Main s'est levee Aëliz* (no. 8a) is a *chanson de rencontre* or encounter song. It is an offshoot of the pastourelle, setting the vibrant maiden Aelis, who has risen early and is gathering flowers in an erotically charged garden where her sensual appeal, held only loosely in check for her long-delayed lover, meanwhile attracts the attention of an unidentified but apparently not unwelcome witness. The song opens in the manner of a well-known cluster of pieces devoted to the archetypal figure of Aelis; however, it veers in stanza 2 away from Aelis, in particular, and becomes a rather all-purpose textual vehicle for music, centered on a generic "she." This loss of specific thematic identity is underlined by the absence of a concluding refrain, a marked departure from other compositions developing the Aelis motif. The fact that stanza 2 is evidently an exogenous, apocryphal addition accounts for this discrepancy. For more on the textual dissonances, disparities in versification, and refrain discontinuity apparent in this song, see Saint-Cricq 2019 and "Reworking into Song" under "Music and Text in the Works of Robert de Reims," below.

The final piece in Robert's extant repertory, *Ja mais, por tant con l'ame el cors me bate* (no. 9), is his single known contribution to the genre of the *sotte chanson contre Amours* (or "silly song against Love"), parodying the ostensibly heartfelt outpourings typical of high-register songs of courtly love. In fact, Robert's lone contribution is the first known example of the genre—of which he may as readily as not have been the very creator. All here is exaggeration and laughter, innuendo and irony, from the first-person singer's peerless love to his lady's dubious profession. It is barbed but probably good-spirited entertainment, whether at court or town square or knightly casern.

Language

The following remarks on language concern only the work of the copyist of *X*, which reflects the usage to be expected of a thirteenth-century trouvère active in the region of Central Old French.[12]

The manuscript reveals a number of inconsistencies in spelling, many of which occur on the same folio. These may be due either to scribal error or to indifference; it is clear that they do not represent phonetic distinctions. Such inconsistency is most notably reflected in rhyme words, which frequently appear in varied graphic form. For example:

- Song no. 2   *-ele* rhymes with *-elle*
- Song no. 4a   *-oir* rhymes with *-oi*
                                 -or rhymes with *-ors*
- Songs nos. 6 and 7a   *-ant* rhymes with *-ent*
- Song no. 8a   *-iz* rhymes with *-is*
                            -ant rhymes with *-ans* and *-enz*

In addition, many such apparent graphic inconsistencies occur in nonrhyming position, as in the following selected instances of subject pronouns:

- 1st pers. sing. *je* 1/1.6 but *g'en* 1/3.2
- 3rd pers. fem. sing. *el* 1/1.2 but *ele* 2/1.2

The absence of a graphic distinction in the following instances precludes the occurrence of any phonetic distinction beween *-o-* and *-ou-*:

- *nouvele* 2/1.2 but *renovele* 2/1.4
- *douz* 4a/1.1 but *doz* 4a/3.8
- *Amors* 3/1.9 but (rhyming) *dolours* 3/1.10 but *dolor* 5a/1.4
- *souvent* 3/4.1 but *corage* 3/4.2
- *souz* 5a/3.12 but *soz* 8a/1.9

The following forms are similarly interchangeable:

- substantives
  bois 5a/3.14 but *bos* 5a/3.13
- prepositions
  sans 2/3.3 but *sanz* 2/4.3
- possessive adjectives
  vo 5a/2.7 but *vostre* 5a/3.4
- verbs
  2nd pers. imperative *donés* 5a/3.3 but *laissiez* 5a/3.5
  2nd pers. present *avés* 5a/3.9 but *avez* 5a/2.6
  3rd pers. present *vet* 2/1.3 but *va* 2/1.5 but *vait* 2/2.6
  3rd pers. future *iert* 2/3.4 but *ert* 4a/2.13
  3rd pers. imperfect *chantoit* 8a/1.6 but *menot* 6/1.3

Note that rhymes in song no. 6 make it clear that the imperfect ending *-ot* is intended as distinct from the imperfect ending in *-oi-*.

In the matter of grammatical case, there are few examples of apparent error. These may be due, as in *mort* 1/1.5 and 4a/3.14, to scribal inattention or to the gradual breakdown of the two-case system—or, as in *traïs* 1/1.2 or *raconté* 2/5.5, to the need to maintain rhyme endings.

A word about *amor(s)*: the difference between the form ending in *-s* and the form with no flexional ending seems to bear no relation to case, number, or gender. The noun is in a class of its own, the difference between the two forms due, most exceptionally, only to the expression or not of personification. Final *-s* betokens personification; all other functions are expressed by the bare form.

Versification: Strophic Structures, Rhyme and Other Phonic Echoes

The thirteen pieces in the lyric corpus attributed to Robert de Reims—nine chansons and the attendant motets of four of them—offer a notable display of compositional skill and creativity. This is particularly true of the motets, a genre that here, as elsewhere, is open to an expanse of poetic freedom, irregularity, and inventiveness that is quite different from the rather constrained formalism of the chanson. The relative characteristics of the two types are implicit in the summary tables presented below.

Table 3A shows the organization of syllable count (meter) and rhyme of each line of the thirteen-piece corpus, arranged across the page. The vertical axis shows the sequence of the pieces within the edition. The numbers at the top of the page represent the lines available for each of the compositions; the maximum number of lines found in the corpus is fifteen.

Table 3B presents the same data, now arranged not by order within the corpus but by syllable count (meter), going vertically from the lowest syllable count in each initial verse to the highest. The relevant occurrences in the corpus are indicated on the right side of the page. Italics indicate refrains and quotations.

Considerable variation is evident first of all in *stanza length*—that is, the number of lines constituting a given stanza. These range through the thirteen texts from as few as 7 (nos. 2 and 9) and 8 (no. 1) to 10 (no. 3), 12 (no. 8), 13 (no. 6), 14 (no. 7), and even 15 (nos. 4 and 5). Note that there is no distinction here between chansons and attendant motets. Note too that the corpus shows no correlation between stanza length and the order of the pieces in the collection; from text to text, there is no stanza-length predictability. It is true, in any case, that the shortest stanzas are those occurring in chansons without corresponding motets, and the longest in chansons with attendant ones.

Like stanza length, *line length*, measured in syllables, shows broad variation and, again, no correlation with manuscript placement. With one exception, pieces that appear only as chansons are homometric: no. 1 composed only of six-syllable lines, nos. 2 and 9 only of ten-syllable lines, and no. 3 only of seven-syllable lines. The exception occurs in no. 6, which stands out for its remarkably inventive metrical breadth, including lines of 7, 1, 5, 2, and 3 syllables. That is usually the sort of freewheeling treatment of meter found in this collection only in chansons with attendant motets. Thus, no. 4 contains lines that are 7, 5, 1, 3, 4, and 6 syllables long; no. 5 is somewhat more restrained, with lines including only 7, 5, 6, and 8 syllables; no. 8 is similarly limited in its heterometric reach, with lines that are only 7, 5, 4, and 6 syllables; but no. 7 displays the same metrical expansiveness seen in no. 4, that is, combining lines of 7, 10, 9, 8, 5, and 6 syllables. Interestingly, all these imaginative sequences begin with a heptasyllable and only then move off in different directions. As table 3B shows, Robert had a clear predilection for opening stanzas with a heptasyllabic foot.

A similar observation may be made in relation to *line scansion*—that is, the arrangement of the metrical units, or syllabic feet, constituting a given line. Again, chanson no. 6 behaves here with a freedom of movement foreign to the compositions that have no attendant motets. Within those that are so paired, the metric arrangements of the various pieces show significant differences from one to another; the tables make this quite clear, just as they do the freedom with which Robert uses third (c) and even fourth (d) rhymes.

Viewed together, these three measures of formal variation—and all the more obviously when the play of masculine and feminine rhymes and the occasional occurrence of unpaired rhyme words are taken into account—lead to the striking observation that no composition in this entire edition of Robert de Reims duplicates any other: in other words, each and every text is a unique composition. It is no less the case, however, that the versification schemes of chansons nos. 1, 2, 3, and 6 occur as well in compositions by other trouvères: (no. 1) Conon de Béthune and Audefroi le Bastart; (no. 2) Gautier d'Espinal, Moniot d'Arras, Thibaut de Champagne, Comte de Bar, and four others, unidentified; (no. 3) Gontier de Soignies; (no. 6) Gilles le Vinier. The versification scheme of chanson no. 9 occurs nowhere else. Strikingly, all four chansons that come from motets—nos. 4, 5, 7, and 8—are schematically unique. Be it noted as well that the trouvères responsible for contrafacta are generally associated with Artois, which corroborates what is said in our Introduction about the circle of influence of Robert de Reims.

The corpus is marked by a ***wide range of homophonic devices***—verbal recurrences taking the form of not only the various types of end rhyme but internal rhyme and alliteration as well. Such echoes thread through the texts as an unsystematized companion to end rhyme, reinforcing the music of the chansons and motets with the musicality of unformalized auditory repetitions. With no regularity of occurrence, such phonic echoes, unlike actual rhymes, have no rhythmic function, but they do contribute, and potently, to the texture of Robert's work.

INTERNAL ECHO

Internal echo is an obvious expression of such verbal music. It is, in fact, a hallmark not only of Robert's stylistic originality but also of his influence on contemporary and later trouvères. His intensive use of echo rhyming in particular, as in nos. 4 and 6, is a notable innovation, emulated by such figures as Gilles le Vinier and Gautier de Coinci, and with an influence extending even into the early fourteenth century.[13]

Internal echo may take various forms, sometimes occurring as whole-word repetition. Here are some examples:

Linking an internal word with the rhyme at the end of the same line, as in:

- no. 3/2.3 *Amors* linked to *amere*

- no. 4a/2.1 *regart* linked to *remir*
- no. 7a/1.11 *doné* linked to *don*

Linking an internal or a line-initial word with the rhyme ending of an earlier line, as in:

- no. 1/3.1 *Pris* linked to 2.8 *pris*
- no. 2/1.4 *renovele* linked to 1.2 *nouvele*
- no. 4a/1.7 *Mir* linked to 1.6 *joïr*; 1.9 *Tir* linked to 1.8 *repentir*; 1.11 *N'assentir* linked to 1.10 *sentir*
- no. 5a/3.5 *Si* linked to 3.4 *merci*
- no. 7a/2.3 *les servirai* linked to 2.1 *servies les ai*
- no. 6/1.2 *Pestre* linked to 1.1 *champestre*; in fact, this chanson, like no. 4a, exemplified above, is replete with examples of shadowing of an earlier word; if the two are both rhymes, the phenomenon is known as "echo rhyming."

Establishing a wholly internal homophonic pair, independent of line-end rhyme, as in:

- no. 2/2.2 *cuer* and 2.3 *cuers*; 3.6 *la mort* and 3.7 *amor*
- no. 3/4.1 *Souvent* repeated

Establishing a network of phonic echoes that, beyond any other device, are marked by the insistent alliteration that they have in common: consider no. 5a, above all, which, beginning with two instances of "d"—1.4 *dolor* and 1.5 *destor*, continues with "t"—1.12 *tint* and *tabor*, "s"—1.13 *sans sejor*, and then with an abundance of instances of "v" spread through all three stanzas with increasing frequency: *(ri)vage, vi, Vers, voie, vi* in stanza 1; *voloir, vostre, (a)vez, vo (de)vis, vos, vis* in stanza 2; and in stanza 3, *vos, Vostre, vostre, vostre, vos, vueill, (a)vés, vos, vos*, which blossoms at last into *le bois vert et flori*.

Among similar alliterative echoes are those in no. 9, which presents three instances of "m"—3.1 *Merveilles m'ai (con)ment* and, in the same line, two instances of "t"—*tant tenue*. Occurrences of "t" have already appeared in 2.6—*tant . . . trovee*, but no alliteration is more striking in the first two stanzas of no. 9 than that of [k], written either as "qu" or as "c": *con, cors, quier, Quant, que, que, (En)cor, que, que, qui, quit, que, cuer, con (Es)cos, qui, contree, coverture, clou, que, cui, color.*

RHYME AND EQUIVALENT LINE-END FEATURES
In both melody and rhythm, the verbal musicality of Robert's compositions is, of course, effected principally by end rhyme or, simply, rhyme. Numerous examples demonstrate

that musicality is often enhanced through the use of rhymes that go beyond the minimal recurrence of a final vowel alone (V), as in *honie / amie* in no. 1/1.1 and 1.3, or the slightly fuller recurrence of final vowel and consonant (VC), as in *dis / mis* in no. 1/2.2 and 2.5. Such larger rhyming units may include the repetition of three phonemes, as in CVC *venir / espanir* in no. 4a/1.1 and 1.3, VCV *bonté / donté* in no. 2/5.1 and 5.6; or more, as in VCVC *repentir / sentir* in no. 4a/1.8 and 1.10; or even more, as in VVCVC *paiement / delaiement* in no. 2/4.5 and 4.6; etc. These rhymes all represent increasingly complex grades of homophony, each, strictly speaking, with its own technical appellation in French (which is the terminology used in the presentation of the versification data in the critical apparatus); here, we use the term "rich rhyme" inclusively to denote all instances beyond V and VC. An inventory of the various rhyme types found in Robert's chansons and motets is presented in table 3C, which offers ready comparison of frequency across the corpus.

There are many places where Robert plays with rhyme beyond the bounds of such standard sequences. His rhymes sometimes traverse word boundaries, as in no. 2/1.1 *en chantant* and 1.3 *enchantant*. Another rhyming game involves pairing a brief word that is identical to the final syllable of a polysyllabic word, absent any etymological association; these are the rhymes often called paronymic, as in:

- no. 1/1.1 *amie* and 1.6 *mie*; 1.4 *vis* and 1.5 *avis*
- no. 5a/3.5 *berchier* and 3.6 *chier*
- no. 9/3.3 *rue* and 3.7 *charrue*

No song makes greater use of this rhyming device than no. 6, whose every stanza includes several instances of such pairing, highlighted whenever the line is only one or two syllables long.

Elsewhere, there are echoes, or partial recurrences, produced through derivation— that is, by polysyllabic words related to simple forms through affixation. Most of Robert's texts show instances of this feature, as in:

- no. 3/3.1 *aventure* linked to 3.5 *Mesaventure*
- no. 9/1.1 *bate* linked to 1.7 *esbate*

It is instructive to note a few other rhyming devices, often associated with the ludic nature of motet composition, that do **not** appear in Robert's works—for example, double rhymes, as in *nule raison / nule mesprison*, or, more expansively, *sert s'amie / servie / sert mie*. Note that double rhymes might accommodate interruption, as in *en trait / s'en retrait* or *m'a asseguré / m'a assené*, as well as the crossing of word boundaries in sequences somewhat more daring than Robert's no. 2, cited above; consider, for example, such oddities as *m'as mis / amis,* or *prison / pris hom*, or *on l'ot / c'on le lot* (these examples all come from the motets in the Chansonnier de Noailles).[14] Also unused by

Robert is the imperfect rhyming device of assonance—that is, lines ending in the same vowel followed by different consonants, as in the pair *espine / prise*.

Oddly, in a corpus that gives so much space to the enhancement of musicality through rich rhyme and other echoing devices, there are two texts that include unrhymed lines, that is, metrically correct verses that end in words without rhyming partners; nos. 4a and 5a have such occurrences (noted as *x* and *y*). Irregularities in meter as well as rhyme are present in the second stanza of song no. 8a. The case of no. 7a reflects a distinct type of variance: both meter and rhyme in the apparent quotations diverge from the rest of the stanza, as is often the case in a *chanson avec des refrains*. These anomalies, be it noted, are found only in chansons that have attendant motets, where unrhymed lines are not uncommon. Other possible explanations for such exceptionality are discussed in "Reworking into Song" under "Music and Text in the Works of Robert de Reims," below.

In sum, the lyric texts of Robert de Reims exhibit great deftness; they display exemplary poetic acuity and homophonic techniques, including some not specifically recognized in this brief sketch of his versification.

Music and Text in the Works of Robert de Reims

Robert's corpus, albeit generically homogeneous as it appears in the songbooks, actually covers two distinct layers: first, five genuine trouvère chansons (nos. 1, 2, 3, 6, 9); second, four polyphonic motets (nos. 4b, 5b, 7b, 8b), later rewritten as monophonic songs (nos. 4a, 5a, 7a, 8a) by a different hand. The corpus thus brings together dissimilar poetico-musical pieces created through different compositional processes by separate writers working within their own chronological framework. The result is that in order to understand this corpus it is essential to study it in two phases, starting here with the five "true" chansons.

THE FIVE GENUINE SONGS
Poetico-Musical Structures
Robert's five genuine trouvère songs appear marked by classicism in regard to their poetico-musical structures. They are in line with the formal categories defined by Dante in his *De vulgari eloquentia*: three show the pattern *pedes cum cauda* (AAB in songs nos. 2, 3*U*, 3*R*, and 9*M*; AAA′B in song no. 9*T*),[15] or the form *pedes cum versibus* in alternative musical versions of these songs (AABB′ in no. 3*T*; AABB in no. 3*X*, see example 1). Two songs are in *oda continua* (nos. 1 and 6), one of which (no. 1) shows a clear distinction between parts A and B (see example 2 and analysis, below).

Example 1. Analysis of song no. 3 in *X*

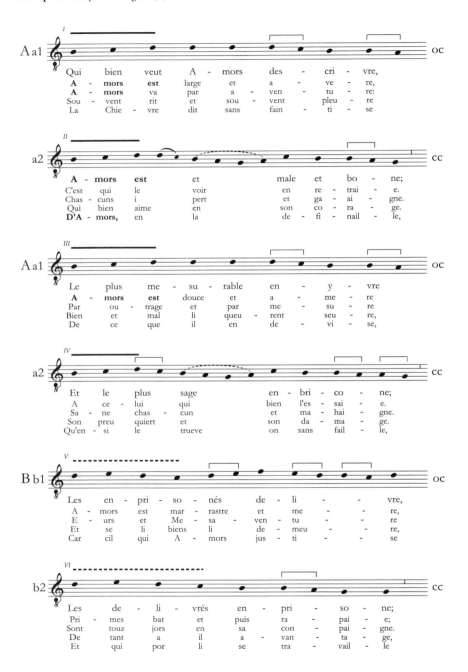

Example 1. Analysis of song no. 3 in *X* (continued)

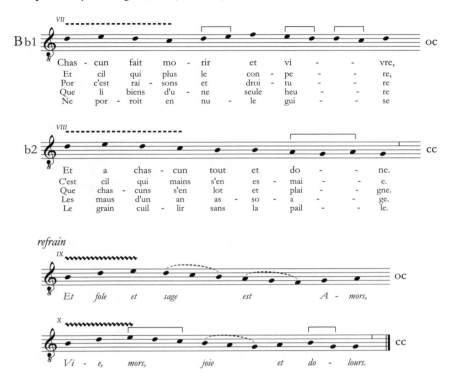

The repetition of the poetico-melodic material of the patterns proceeds in a custom-ary manner: *pedes* AA are organized around two isometric verse phrases a1 and a2 repeated in alternation; the four lines are organized in alternate rhymes, which allows for the convergence of the repeated musical sonorities with the repeated verse sonori-ties (see *pedes* AA in example 1). *Versus* BB in song no. *3X* is arranged in the same way (example 1). Cadential treatments converge in marking the phrasings and cæsuræ of the patterns AAB or AABB, with songs nos. *3TUX* and *9M* alternating, for example, the open cadences in a1 and the closed cadences in a2 (marked respectively "oc" and "cc" in example 1); no. *3X* behaves similarly between b1 and b2 of the *versus* (example 1). The treatment of the approximately octave-wide range of the five pieces also contrib-utes subtly to the design of their form. The melody may show an arclike development, moving from the beginning of the work to the middle, from the first fifth of the octave toward the last fourth, then reversing its direction at the end of the song (nos. 1 and *3TUX*; see example 1 for the version in *X*). This path allows for a contrast among the various parts: in no. *3T*, the *pedes* AA essentially cluster around the fifth g-d′ (phrases I–IV), while the *cauda* opens on the fourth d′-g′ (V to VII) before gradually returning to the initial situation (VIII to X). The treatment of the range leaves room in other cases for the introduction of a contrast between *pedes* phrases a1 and a2 (see I–IV in songs nos. 2, 3*R*, 9*MT*); the contrast is particularly effective when these phrases are additionally set between ascendant and descendant movements (no. 2, I / III vs. II / IV), or inversely (no. 9*T*).

Repetition, Transposition, Variation, Amplification

In addition to the large-scale poetico-musical repetition due to the formal categories at issue, Robert's chansons are intricately wrought through a subtle play of melodic recurrences and development based on four techniques: strict repetition, transposed repetition, variation, and amplification. These techniques allow for the recall of motifs or phrases across the various parts of the songs. Thus, in no. 2, the last two phrases develop the first two in reverse order: phrase VI is an amplification of II, while phrase VII is an amplification of I. Likewise, song no. 9*T* is traversed by the repetition of a four-note descending leap of a minor seventh (motif f′ d′ b g in the middle of phrases I, III, V, and as the incipit of VII), reversed by a five-note (motif g b d′ e′ f′ in II and IV) or a three-note (g e′ f′ in VII) ascending leap of a minor seventh. Such reiterations also make possible the melodic cohesion peculiar to each part. Thus, part AA of no. 3*TUX* repeats the same incipit b c′ d′ in its four initial phrases (motifs topped by a solid line in example 1). Likewise, in no. 3*R*, the opening motif of phrases II and IV is a repetition, transposed to the upper fifth, of the motif of phrases I and III.

Song no. 1, though not based on a repetitive type of structure, provides an excellent example of those forms tightly hemmed by cadences, treatment of range, and the techniques of melodic development (see example 2). From a textual point of view, the song divides into two parts, A and B, four lines each, as suggested by syntax and meaning—with two separate statements—as well as versification, with its four lines of alternate rhymes in A, then enclosed in B. The cadential scheme corroborates this pattern, for each part shows three phrases with open cadences, followed by a final phrase with a concluding cadence (marked "oc" and "cc," respectively). The ambitus d-d′ in part A stretches up to f′ in part B (phrase VI) before shrinking back in the last phrase. The play of melodic development contributes to the structuring of the piece. The repetition of the same cadence (motif topped by a line arrow) coordinates phrases VI and VII. The incipit of phrase I is repeated in VI and transposed in IV and VIII (motifs topped by a solid line). Likewise, a single transposed cadence combines phrases III and IV before reappearing at the end of the piece (motifs topped by a dotted line). Parts A and B are further related to each other through the amplification of phrases I and II into VI and VII (phrases marked 1 and 2 in the example); the incipit of phrases II and VII is also transposed at V (motifs topped by a wavy line). Finally, in a clear decision to make the parts symmetrical, the final phrase of part B repeats the last phrase of part A (phrases marked 3).

Example 2. Analysis of song no. 1 in *X*

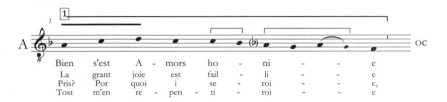

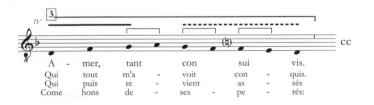

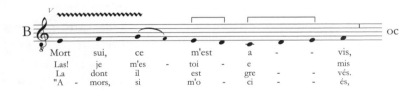

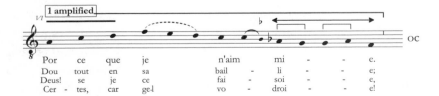

Example 2. Analysis of song no. 1 in *X* (continued)

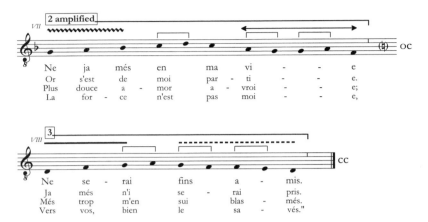

	Ne	ja	més	en	ma	vi	-	-	e
	Or	s'est	de	moi	par	-	ti	-	-	e.
	Plus	douce	a	-	mor	a	-	vroi	-	-	e;
	La	for	-	ce	n'est	pas	moi	-	-	e,

	Ne	se	-	rai	fins	a	-	mis.
	Ja	més	n'i	se	-	rai	pris.
	Més	trop	m'en	sui	blas	-	més.
	Vers	vos,	bien	le	sa	-	vés."

The Collaboration of Music and Text

From the point of view of declamation, the style of Robert de Reims's chansons is customary for this genre: with the exception of the strict syllabism of song no. 6, the music presents the text in a globally syllabic manner, with melismas placed generally at line end (nos. 1, 2, 3*RTUX*, 9*MT*), at the beginning (nos. 2, 9*T*), and at the cæsura (no. 3*TUX*).

The relation of text to music in Robert's songs is more notable in the coordination effected between their respective melodic and homophonic devices. This relation may manifest itself in the recurrence of the same verse sonorities at identical musical locations right through the several stanzas. Thus, in no. 2, between the homologous verses of stanzas 3 and 4, rhymes on three syllables occur on the same musical cadence at the end of every phrase ("vraiement" / "-saiement", "-aïe" / "-vaïe", etc.); furthermore, phrase VII shows an initial verse repetition between stanzas 3 and 4, therefore occurring on the same music, with "Que bone amor" becoming "Ont bone amor." Yet more significant is the fact that these correspondences may occur as repetitions within a given stanza. Still in no. 2, the identical cadences of phrases I and III bring equivocal three-syllable rhymes in stanza 1 ("en chantant" / "enchantant"), disyllabic and trisyllabic rhymes in stanzas 2 and 3, respectively, an identical four-syllable rhyme on "essaiement" in stanza 4, and finally a disyllabic rhyme in stanza 5. Likewise, the identical musical cadence of phrases II and IV shows the paronymous rhyme "nouvele" / "renovele" in stanza 1. Song no. 3*TUX* shows a coordination of verse and musical elements around an instance of anaphora. The musical anaphora of phrases I to IV (see example 1 for the version in *X*, motifs topped by a solid line) is paired with a verse anaphora that is set both between the different stanzas and within a single stanza: "Amors est" is, in fact, repeated at the beginning of line 2 in stanza 1 and at the start of lines 1 and 3 in stanza 2, with "Amors" occurring again at the incipit of line 1 in stanza 3 and line 2 in stanza 5 (see the words in bold in example 1).

Song no. 6 offers the most remarkable case of collaboration between verse and music. This composition has little in common with the other genuine songs: with its strict syllabism, very limited ambitus, and *oda continua* form showing no distinct parts or precise cadential pattern, no. 6 is wholly focused on the figure of echo in both verse and music. Echo rhymes structure all lines of all stanzas, and in a number of places, echoing extends into the music as well. There is a strict melodic echo supporting the poetic echo "-pestre / Pestre" at the end of phrase I, and the same is true at the end of III ("destre / Estre") and IV ("par semblant / En enblant"). Poetico-musical echo may also be found at some distance: the echo rhymes "-jolot / Et ot" in phrase V are heard on the same musical motifs as the echo rhymes "menot / Et n'ot" in phrase II.

Alternative and Evolutive Versions

Two of Robert's five "genuine" songs, nos. 2 and 9, transmitted with divergent musical versions, have led us to propose several editions for each. In their different musical presentations, the two works show quite separate transmissional logic. The two musical readings of song no. 9—*M* and *T*—are clearly alternative: not only is the musical material different in the two sources, but the musical form—AAB in *M* and AAA′B in *T*—sets the text somewhat differently. It is noteworthy that the musical hand responsible for song no. 9 in *M* is different from the main hand at work on the song collection, whereas the text is due to the usual literary scribe. It is thus plausible that this musical version is a later addition.[16] The case of song no. 3 as it appears in *R* falls within the same transmissional process: having nothing in common with the versions of this song in *MTU*, *R*'s reading also constitutes an alternative—and certainly late—version, such as very often occurs in this songbook.

The *TUX* versions of no. 3 suggest a different sort of transmission: these are evolutive rather than alternative, and the musical material lets us distinguish between permanent and unstable strata between the versions. The stable material is essentially localized in the *pedes* (I–IV); phrases I and III are quite stable in *T*, *U*, and *X*, differentiated only by a slightly varying cadential movement before reaching the final a. Phrases II to IV are similar, though subject to greater variance in their way of conjoining incipit to explicit. Significantly, the three versions preserve the anaphora at the beginning of the four phrases, the importance of which for the poem was noted above.[17] *Cauda* (phrases V–VIII in *U*) or *versus* (V–VIII in *TX*) are, on the contrary, the locus of recomposition of the musical material between the versions. To be sure, certain elements are similar, such as the cadence characterized by repeated notes (end of VI and VII in *U*, VI in *X*, VI and VIII in *T*) and the initial sudden contrast in the range at the beginning of part B

Example 3. Phrases V and VI (beginning of part B) of song no. 3 in *U*

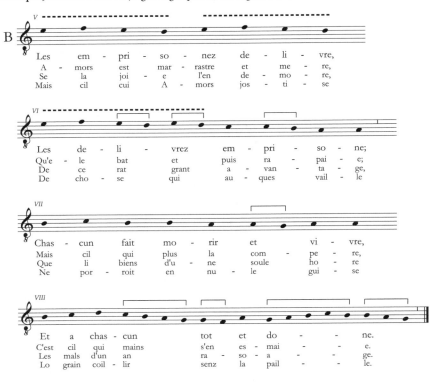

V

Les em - pri - so - nez de - li - vre,
A - mors est mar - rastre et me - re,
Se la joi - e l'en de - mo - re,
Mais cil cui A - mors jos - ti - se

VI

Les de - li - vrez em - pri - so - ne;
Qu'e - le bat et puis ra - pai - e;
De ce rat grant a - van - ta - ge,
De cho - se qui au - ques vail - le

VII

Chas - cun fait mo - rir et vi - vre,
Mais cil qui plus la com - pe - re,
Que li biens d'u - ne soule ho - re
Ne por - roit en nu - le gui - se

VIII

Et a chas - cun tot et do - - ne.
C'est cil qui mains s'en es - mai - - e.
Les mals d'un an ra - so - a - - ge;
Lo grain coil - lir senz la pail - - le.

(phrases V–VI in all three versions). However, in the second part, a visible phenomenon of recomposition underlies the passage from *U* to *X*: the repeated motif that constrains phrases V and VI in *U* (example 3, motifs topped by a dotted line) is shown as recomposed in *X*, transposed to the lower second and used in the incipit of phrases V to VIII (see example 1, motifs topped by a dotted line) in order to restore the principle of anaphora of phrases I–IV. If this material does not appear in *T*, *T* does, nevertheless, share with *X* the formal project of a second section built as a *versus*, unequally executed in the two readings: *T* and *X* both show a phrase V repeated in VII, but where *X* has a new strict repetition of VI to VIII (see example 1), *T* prefers melodic variety.

These evolutive changes in no. 3 are no doubt to be understood within a chronological framework. The part of songbook *U* that preserves this work is remarkably early,[18] probably close to the period of its composition, whereas *T* is surely a source copied in the 1270s, and *X* may well date from the years 1270 to 1280.[19] It is thus tempting to see such recomposition as a gradual evolution of Robert's work, refashioned by orality, the hand of various copyists, or the intervention of later performers or trouvères. Refrain

Example 4. Phrases IV, VIII, and final refrain of song no. 3 in *T*

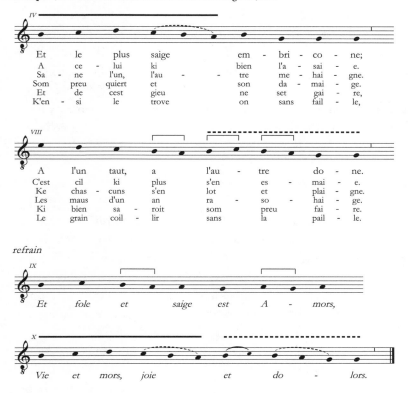

vdB 710, presented in *T* and *X* at the end of every stanza, bears telling witness to this manner of gradual recomposition. The refrain does not occur in the early version in *U*, which is apparently not a matter of forgetfulness: we have only to notice the melismatic dilatation of the final phrase VIII and of its cadence to identify it as a peroration, all the more clearly so, as it is an amplification of phrases II and IV, which is already the end of part AA of the work. This refrain, which has no known concordance, was surely added to the later copies. The appending of the refrain to *TX* (and *R* too) is, besides, obvious through its melodic instability—the three versions offering different melodies—and particularly the divergent strategies by which each very clearly seeks to tie the melody of the couplet to the preexisting song. In *X*, the melodic material used for the refrain has nothing in common with the rest of the song (see example 1); on the other hand, it reproduces the principle of musical anaphora stemming from part AA (see solid lines) and BB (see dotted lines) by introducing a new anaphoric motif at the beginning of each line of the couplet (see wavy lines), a distich that moreover reproduces the alternation between open and closed cadences that prevails throughout the composition.

The version in *T* proceeds contrariwise: the music provided for the refrain does not lead back to the use of anaphora in the song but rather repeats the melodic material of the work (see example 4): the first half of the final line repeats the first part of phrases II and IV (solid lines), while the second half echoes the cadence of phrase VIII (dotted lines). Obvious here are the two different logics governing the recomposition of the material coming from the song: the refrain in *X* makes use of the compositional procedures in the song rather than its melodic material to ensure the unity of song and refrain, whereas *T* makes use of the melodic material—but not the procedure—to ensure the coherence of the entire work.

THE FOUR MOTETS AND THEIR ATTENDANT SONGS
Hallmarks of the Motet
The four remaining pieces (nos. 4, 5, 7, and 8) are works essentially different from the five "genuine" songs, as much in their poetico-musical fabric as in their compositional procedures. Indeed, as demonstrated in Saint-Cricq 2019,[20] these four works were originally polyphonic motets composed by Robert de Reims (our nos. 4b, 5b, 7b, and 8b) and then turned into strophic trouvère songs (our nos. 4a, 5a, 7a, and 8a) at a later stage by an anonymous continuator. This was done by the time of the great compilatory project *KNPX*—the only sources available for these "chansonized" motets.

As it most often appears in the thirteenth century, the motet may be defined as a polyphonic work in two to four parts, built on a preexisting liturgical chant placed in the lower voice; this is the "tenor." All the parts are measured according to thirteenth-century modal theory, with the upper voice carrying a nonstrophic text, in either Latin or French. When a motet includes more than one upper voice, it is most often polytextual. The vast majority of motets are copied in liturgical polyphonic collections or in specific motet books. The four motets composed by Robert are two-voiced, with no. 4b also appearing with a third part in two sources. They are recorded anonymously in the sources, as was customary in the polyphonic repertory. The upper voices of these motets present the same melody and text as their corresponding songs; note, however, that motet no. 5b is today preserved only as a Latin contrafact of the now-lost French version that is presented in this edition (see Commentary on no. 5b). Two of our four motets (nos. 4b and 5b) also appear as later clausulæ—that is, *sine littera* polyphonic pieces for liturgical use during the Mass or the Office. In this presentation, the upper voice carries the same music as its attendant song but does not retain the text; rather, the upper part is sung on the same syllable(s) as its tenor.

The generic origin of nos. 4, 5, 7, and 8 is crucial as regards the poetico-musical makeup of these pieces. As noted earlier (see "Versification"), the four pieces stand apart from the genuine songs with respect to stanza length, line length, line scansion, and the presence of unmatched rhymes; rather, they are defined by the versification style proper to the motet. The melodic morphology and the formal design of the four works are also much more typical of the motet—a genre customarily marked by heteromelism and heterometry—than of the chanson. Indeed, only composition no. 5 is structured according to the *pedes cum cauda* pattern, whereas the three other pieces exhibit neither the large-scale poetico-musical repetitions of formal types nor the subtle play of melodic recurrences and development already pointed out in Robert's five genuine songs. The four works show neither the careful treatment of the range nor the subtle balance of the phrases found in the true songs. No. 8, with its complex turns and its ill-conjoined profile backed to a small ambitus, is symptomatic of a voice stemming from the motet. Rather than the formal types and melodic development that craft classic trouvère chansons in general and Robert's five songs in particular, our four pieces make use of the stereotypical melodic motifs shared by the diverse polyphonic settings built on the same tenor. For example, the beginnings of nos. 5 and 7 are typical of the formulæ found at the incipit of other motets and clausulæ built on the tenor DOMINO QUONIAM.[21]

Also quite typical of the motet is the intertextual cohesion between the texts of the upper parts and the liturgical and scriptural context of the tenor. Motets nos. 5b and 7b, with their tenor stemming from *Hec dies V Confitemini domino quoniam bonus*, present a typical picture of secular motets constructed on this gradual and its host Psalm 117: the theme of divine mercy gives way to a recasting in which the lover implores the pity of the loved or desired woman, who in turn grants him her amorous or erotic mercy.[22] While the narrator implores the shepherdess in no. 5b, the narrator of no. 7b even uses the terms of the psalm to supplicate the lady to grant a secular sort of gratification (line 13). In motet no. 8b, the Alleluia whence came the tenor sung for the Ordinary of the Virgins is the perfect stage for the character of Aelis, providing a classic juxtaposition of the sacred and secular figurations of maidenhood; moreover, the word MANSUETUDINEM ("gentleness") offers a perfect lexical context for the intimate words and atmosphere of the motetus text. Finally, Psalm 44, the source of the tenor text, is one of the biblical writings that make use of the imagery of the heavenly marriage, and adequately sets the scene for the maiden's sensuality and desire heard in the upper voice. This sensuality is pervasive in the work, whose motifs of awakening and entering an orchard constitute suggestive episodes.

Reworking into Song

The songs attendant to motets are the fruits of a complex process of recomposition: not only were the upper voices of the motets stripped of their tenor (as occasionally seen in other song collections),[23] but the original motet texts also came to be enhanced with supplementary stanzas. In grafting these additional stanzas onto the motets, the continuator clearly was attempting to conceal that generic source as much as possible and to turn Robert's motets into organically genuine chansons. However, despite the continuator's effort, the resulting songs bear the mark of their generic origin and produce unusual, heterogeneous, and sometimes problematic compositions.

The reworking that converts motets into songs is visible through the collection's numerous instances of mismatch between initial stanzas and those that follow. The discontinuity can be thematic, as in song no. 8a. Its first stanza—and therefore the text of the originating motet—was crafted by someone perfectly familiar with, and mindful of, the Aelis archetype, incorporating its customary motifs of waking early, entering into an orchard, and gathering flowers. In that respect, the second stanza is clearly dissonant: Aelis is replaced by an impersonal "she." The typical Aelis motifs give way to a long, stereotypical physical description (lines 1–8), of the sort often brooded about in chansons and motets, but alien to any other work staging Aelis.[24]

The versification of the song versions is also revealing of this process of recomposition, showing an obvious discontinuity between the original text of the motet and the new stanzas of the song. At the least problematic level, the added stanzas always show rhyme schemes different from the original ones, and sometimes even a different number of rhymes (nos. 4a and 5a). Furthermore, disparity in rhyme quality frequently appears between the original and subsequent stanzas. For instance, in chanson no. 8a, stanza 2 offers no more than two separated leonine rhymes (in lines 4 and 11), contrasting with the four leonine rhymes (lines 1 and 2, then lines 10 and 12), the two rich rhymes (lines 6 and 7), and the two *rimes batelées* (lines 2 and 3) of stanza 1. The most telling breach arises in the echo rhymes in no. 4a, which are absent from stanza 2 and only partly present in stanza 3, where they are reintroduced in lines 6–7 and 8–9, but not in lines 10–11.

Striking metrical incoherencies within the added stanzas negatively affect the text/music relationship crafted in the original material. Thus, in stanzas 2–3 of song no. 5a, the feminine rhymes of stanza 1 become masculine (lines 1, 3, and 6), thereby filling the equivalent of seven notes instead of eight with the effacement of the unstressed final -*e* (see example 5, with line ends in bold); the final notes of these phrases thus remain unused in stanzas 2–3. In order to compensate for the shortening of lines 1, 3, and 6, the continuator lengthened the lines that follow (2, 4, and 7) by giving each an extra syllable; in so doing, he rendered the musical phrases and poetic lines out of phase with one another (see example 5). Likewise, in song no. 4a, the syllable count of lines 12 and 13, respectively heptasyllabic and tetrasyllabic in stanza 1, is reversed in stanza 2; such manipulation reshapes there too the music/text structure of the passage, since the new break in stanza 2 occurs at a point not corresponding to a break in poetry or music in stanza 1.

These few examples of the numerous dissonances between the original layer of the material and the stanzas grafted onto the motets substantiate the notion that the song versions constitute exogenous additions, postdating the composition of the motets by Robert de Reims, and produced by one or more authors hiding behind Robert's

Example 5. Lines 1–7 of stanzas 1–3 of song no. 5a in *X*

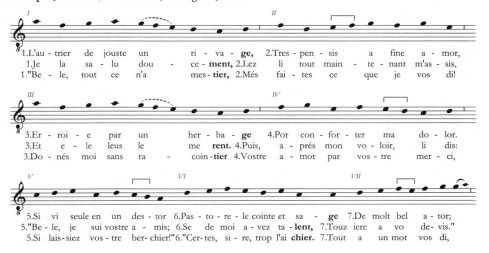

I

1.L'au - trier de jouste un ri - va - **ge,** 2.Tres - pen - sis a fine a - mor,
1.Je la sa - lu dou - ce - **ment,** 2.Lez li tout main - te - nant m'as - sis,
1."Be - le, tout ce n'a mes - **tier,** 2.Més fai - tes ce que je vos di!

III   *IV*

3.Er - roi - e par un her - ba - ge 4.Por con - for - ter ma do - lor.
3.Et e - le leus le me **rent.** 4.Puis, a - prés mon vo - loir, li dis:
3.Do - nés moi sans ra - coin - **tier** 4.Vostre a - mor par vos - tre mer - ci,

V   *VI*   *VII*

5.Si vi seule en un des - tor 6.Pas - to - re - le cointe et sa - **ge** 7.De molt bel a - tor;
5."Be - le, je sui vostre a - mis; 6.Se de moi a - vez ta - **lent,** 7.Touz iere a vo de - vis."
5.Si lais - siez vos - tre ber - chier!" 6."Cer - tes, si - re, trop l'ai **chier.** 7.Tout a un mot vos di,

attribution in the chansonniers. These four apocryphal songs thus clearly belong to the rich medieval tradition of continuations.

The Trouvère and the Interaction of Motet and Chanson

The case of the four chansons/motets linked to Robert de Reims has significant repercussions for the history of the trouvère chanson and that of the motet, and especially the interaction between these genres. Indeed, the generic crossover between song and motet showcased by Robert's corpus exemplifies a tendency, in the second half of the thirteenth century, to multiply interactions between the chanson and motet repertories. This gradual melding is palpable through the contents and organization of songbooks, with the motet becoming gradually ensconced in trouvère anthologies. Like *X* with Robert's four works, chansonniers *M*, *T*, and *a* also preserve motet voices monophonically within their song collections. *M* and *T* additionally grant motets their own separate section, associating the genre even more firmly with the art of the trouvères. Finally, the classification by rubrics in late chansonniers such as *a* and *I* solidifies the genre as a new standard category of secular lyric: the motets are copied there alongside grands chants, jeux-partis, and pastourelles—and with equivalent status. Such generic fluidity also appears in the very process of composing these works in the thirteenth century. Indeed, the period 1250–1315 saw the characteristics of polyphony and chanson melding with one another in such corpora as, among others, the collections of monophonic motets preserved in chansonniers *N* and *I*, the motets built on monophonic vernacular songs as tenors, and the motets built according to formal types stemming from the chanson.[25]

Finally, the composition of French secular motets by an identified trouvère as early as ca. 1200 is determinant in both the history of the motet and our conception of trouvère art. Robert's four chansons/motets first contribute to altering the traditional narrative regarding the motet genre, said to have been born of the trope of liturgical clausulæ through Latin texts, a history of secularization and vernacularization constituting its further development.[26] With four works starting as French secular motets composed ca. 1200, two of them then turned into liturgical clausulæ incorporating materials originating in the chanson and one also turned into a sacred Latin motet, before all of them were adapted, at last, as multistrophic chansons for a songbook sometime around 1270/1280, Robert's corpus upsets the traditional history of the motet. Furthermore, the identification of a trouvère, nearly eighty years before Adam de la Halle, as a most probable composer of motets enriches our conventional view of the "trouvère" as merely a poet and composer of monophonic lyrics. In fact, Robert de Reims is only one of the fourteen trouvères associated with the motet through the ascription of several motetus voices wandering within song collections in diverse songbooks.[27] The identification of Robert de Reims as a composer of both trouvère song and polyphonic motet therefore may be taken as an indication of broader trouvère involvement in the polyphonic repertory, and may point to the figure of the trouvère as one of the important links in the exchanges and interactions among motet, clausula, and chanson; between vernacular and Latin corpora; and between liturgical and secular genres in the thirteenth century.

Editorial Policy for the Texts and Translations

With the exception of no. 9, the texts of the songs present the redaction transmitted in manuscript X. We have elected X as our base manuscript because it includes most of the songs attributed to Robert de Reims (eight out of nine, more than any other source). Our presentation of the songs as they appear in a single manuscript, and in the order in which they appear in that source, even when the particular version in X may be viewed as "faulty," is meant to reinforce Robert's authorial presence. In our edition, the text and the music are always based on the same manuscript.[28]

In editing the songs and motets, we have generally adhered to the principle of minimal intervention. We have made corrections when demanded by sense, versification, or musical design. We have also emended a few errors apparently due to scribal negligence or inattentiveness in copying, rather than evolving morphological patterns. Hypermetric and hypometric lines are indicated by numbers preceded by a plus (+) or minus (−) sign. For passages marked *missing*, we have taken the reading from another manuscript (identified in parentheses), unless an editorial conjecture is specified. When an emendation other than an evident one is adopted from an earlier edition, credit appears after the rejected reading.

Within the Old French texts, square brackets are used to denote refrains that are unrecorded or only partially recorded in the source. They are not used to indicate editorial conjectures of words or parts of words (unless so specified in the notes), nor are they used when a reading is taken from another manuscript.

Variants list readings that differ from the edited text, not necessarily from the base manuscript. Variants are presented selectively. Orthographic variants, whether reflective of dialectal phonological distinctions (e.g., *le/lou*) or not (e.g., *ke/que*), are excluded. All others are presented, viz., those that in any way affect sense or meter and those that are of morphosyntactic interest, the latter including most notably all instances of variation in case flexion. When a variant reading is found in multiple sources, it appears in the critical apparatus in the orthography of the first manuscript listed.

In the use of accents, we followed the recommendations made in Lepage 2001, 101–5, in addition to those proposed in Foulet and Speer 1979, 67–73. We have regularized the use of *i, j, u*, and *v* in accordance with modern orthography. Abbreviations, including roman numerals, are silently expanded, except that we transcribe final -*x* as *x* in every case, as advised in Foulet and Speer 1979, 63, rather than treat it as an abbreviation, unless otherwise noted in the rejected readings (for example, in the case of *D(i)ex,* and to rectify versification, as in song no. 6, line 3.11). A nasal bar over a vowel is taken to represent *n* in all instances—that is, even before bilabials (*p, b, m*). Enclisis is indicated by an internal period (e.g., *ne·l*).

In the Old French texts of songs, but not motets, capital letters are systematically used in verse-initial position, irrespective of their occurrence in the manuscript. Refrains and quotations are given in italics. We acknowledge quotations for which there are known concordances; normally, we do not recognize those that are as yet only postulated.

Determining the lineation of a nonstrophic text can be challenging inasmuch as motet texts are not bound by fixed form; moreover, we found the scribes' use of the *punctum* to mark the ends of text lines to be inconsistent. Our guiding editorial principle has been to show clearly the metric patterns that we judge to be correct and to make both line-end and internal rhyme apparent on the page. Within the Old French texts, a two-em space is used to reveal internal rhymes.

The aim of our translations is to render the meaning of the texts as faithfully as possible, while giving an accurate sense of the tone of the pieces. We do not intend the translations to be read as English or French poems, rhymed and metrically structured; since their lineation may suggest verse, we have deliberately used lowercase letters at the beginning of lines to signal the fact that these are prose translations. Old French poetry is characterized by its use of a limited number of polysemic, coded terms. Throughout the songs, we have varied English equivalents for a particular Old French term: *douce,* for example, is translated as "sweet" in one instance and as "dear" or "gentle" in others, in order to reflect the wide semantic fields in which these terms function. We have avoided contemporary colloquialisms and have retained terms that pertain to medieval culture (such as "mercy"). Old French syntax can separate relative clauses from their antecedents, use a postpositioned noun subject, omit subject and object pronouns, use pronouns without clear antecedents, or disregard the logical concordance of tenses (notably, move freely between past and present). Had we always reproduced the sentence structure of the original or failed to alter the tense sequence, we would not have been able to provide accessible, nuanced, transparent translations. By conveying a measure of the poetic value of the original, our translations are meant to encourage the reader to examine the original.

Editorial Policy for the Music

SOURCES

For the musical edition of Robert's songs, we chose the same base manuscript as that chosen for his texts—chansonnier X. Two exceptions were nevertheless inevitable. The first is song no. 9, which does not appear in X and for which we selected two chansonniers, M and T, as they show separate melodies for this song. The second exception is song no. 3, for which we used chansonniers R, T, and U along with X, since all four exhibit different readings of the music. Other sources occasionally served in the emendation of flaws in the base manuscript.

No single manuscript served as the base for all the motets. We chose the motet collection W_2 for no. 4b, while Mo served for no. 7b, and N for no. 8b. The case of motet no. 5b stands apart, as we reconstructed the piece from a composition now lost (see Saint-Cricq 2019 and Commentary); while the reconstruction uses chansonnier X for the text, the music comes from a Latin motet contrafact in W_2. The other sources served, when necessary, to emend defective passages in one or another of the base manuscripts.

Other sources occasionally served to elucidate problems in our manuscripts. They offered concordant materials possibly shared by Robert's corpus and another musical source, such as refrains. The sources of these concordances are identified in the section headed "Material."

EDITORIAL APPROACH

In editing both songs and motets, we adhered as closely as possible to the original musical text, respecting its individual traits and avoiding, unless strictly necessary, any normalization or recourse to readings in other sources. While adhering to their base manuscripts, editors sometimes face transmissional questions and instabilities in the works treated; thus, when we encountered a song copied with dissimilar or different melodies across the sources, we chose to offer multiple transcriptions rather than conceal divergences by presenting a single, "authoritative" transcription (nos. 3 and 9).

All our songs are transcribed nonmensurally, as is standard today for such works, giving the repertory rhythmic freedom, and favoring declamatory and ornamental flexibility. All the motets are transcribed mensurally, as is normal in a genre whose parts are all governed by the six rhythmic modes.[29]

TRANSCRIPTIONS OF THE MUSIC

The songs of Robert de Reims are all copied in nonmensural notation across the chansonniers. The sources all exhibit the same basic notational lexicon. The notes may appear as simple notes, ligated notes, plicated notes, and *conjoncturæ* or *currentes*. They are transcribed in our edition according to established modern conventions: ligatures are indicated by horizontal square brackets above the staff (e.g., no. 1, I, on "ho-"); diamond-shaped *conjoncturæ* or *currentes* are rendered by dashed slurs over the notes (e.g., no. 1, VI, on "je"). The unnotated *plica* is signaled as a small note tied to its host pitch by a solid slur, and may be either ascending (e.g., no. 4a, I, end of system) or descending (e.g., no. 1, III, on "a-").

The upper voices of motets in *N* and *W₂*, albeit measured, are copied in these sources in an unmeasured notation and share the same basic lexicon as the songs with which they are paired. In *Mo*, on the other hand, the motets are mensurally notated—that is, with a differentiation between *longa* and *brevis*. As is conventional in this repertory, the double long (*duplex longa*) corresponds to a dotted half note, the ternary long (*longa triorum temporum*) to a dotted quarter, the *longa recta* or *brevis altera* is rendered by a quarter, the *brevis recta* by an eighth, and the *semibrevis* by a sixteenth.

In both motet and song sources, the *tractus* is used to delimit the boundaries of a musical phrase, even possibly corresponding to a measured silence in the case of the motets. It is transcribed as a vertical stroke in the transcriptions (e.g., no. 1, I, end of system). The *tractus* is also used in the sources to signal the end of a work, and in such cases, it is translated in our transcriptions by a final bar line. The range of C and F clefs found in both motet and song sources are all rendered in our edition as a transposing treble clef.

PRESENTATION OF THE WORKS

In our presentation of the songs, we chose to provide one staff per musical phrase, which normally coincides with the poetic line, the pair thus constituting the basic unit of trouvère song structure. There are nevertheless two exceptions. Songs nos. 4a and 6 deploy intensive poetic echoing that sometimes extends to the music; in order to make this compositional feature obvious in the musical edition, we present the short echoing phrases/lines right after the echoed ones, rather than give them their own lines (e.g., no. 4a, VI, end of staff).

The presentation of the motets follows the principles set out in Saint-Cricq et al. 2017. Note that while part designations are never specified in thirteenth-century motet sources, they figure in our transcriptions from bottom to top as tenor and motetus.

The musical edition of the songs and motets reproduces the texts exactly as they are presented in the separate textual edition. However, the diereses sometimes used there to mark the syllabic value of certain vowels are not reproduced in the musical edition, since the distribution of text under the music suffices to distinguish one syllable from another. Italics are used either to signal quotations—that is, a portion of text and/or music that is also found in another work (e.g., no. 4a, end of stanzas 1 and 2)—or to indicate a refrain (e.g., no. 3a, end of each stanza).

The musical editions are keyed to the critical commentary through reference numbers placed above the staff at the beginning of each staff. In the song transcriptions, the roman numerals use phrases/lines as a benchmark, while the arabic numerals in motet transcriptions refer to the unit of the perfection, a ternary long, transcribed as a dotted quarter note or rest in the edition.

EDITORIAL INTERVENTIONS

In both song and motet transcriptions, we followed the principle of minimal intervention. Other sources were used only for passages lacunary in the base manuscript or clearly defective and nonfunctional. In motets nos. 4b and 5b, other polyphonic sources also served to assign a rhythmic mode to the motet. On account of the essential musical differences between the motet (a genre that is measured and polyphonic for the most part) and trouvère song (a genre that is unmeasured and monodic), motet sources were not used to emend the song transcriptions, with the exception of a few faulty or missing passages that could not have been reconstructed otherwise. Song sources were never used in the editing of motets. A few editorial conjectures were necessary in the edition of both songs and motets. Every editorial intervention, whether based on other readings or conjectural, is duly recorded and explained in the "Notes to the Musical Transcription" and sometimes also discussed under "Commentary."

Accidentals are the product of specific editorial interventions. The edition distinguishes between accidentals in the source and editorial accidentals. Source accidentals are signaled as is standard in modern notation—that is, in normal size within the staff (e.g., no. 1, I to III). They remain valid until a natural appears or until a change of system occurs to cancel the accidental by a natural sign in parentheses. Editorial accidentals may be added in two ways: those that apply to a lengthy passage are notated in normal size within the staff in parentheses (e.g., no. 1, V and VI), and those that apply only to a single note are notated above that note (e.g., no. 2, notes 4 to 6). In this edition, treatment of accidentals is oriented toward the emendation of unwanted linear sonorities (and also vertical ones in the motets), taking into account the general recommendations enunciated in thirteenth-century music theory.

Presentation of the Critical Apparatus

FORMAL AND GENERIC CLASSIFICATION
For each composition, we identify the song's lyric type (in the case of a pastourelle, *chanson de rencontre*, and *sotte chanson*), form (in the case of a *chanson à refrain* and *chanson avec des refrains*), and genre (in the case of a motet).

CATALOGUING
Under this rubric, we provide identifying numbers in standard bibliographies: Spanke 1955, Linker 1979, Mölk and Wolfzettel 1972, and van den Boogaard 1969 for the chanson repertory; and Ludwig 1910 for the motets.[30]

MANUSCRIPTS
The first manuscript cited is the base for the edition of the text and music. Other manuscripts (concordances) follow in alphabetical order, all uppercase sigla preceding lowercase sigla. Numbers indicate folios (with the exception of manuscript *K*, which is paginated), and both recto and verso are noted. The presence of music is indicated by two notes (♫). Attributions, if any, are specified in parentheses in the orthography of the manuscript source. The manuscript used as the base for the music is indicated in the edition of the music whenever more than one melody is provided.

MATERIAL
Under this heading, we list all quotations and borrowings found in the songs and motets. This includes textual and/or musical refrains shared with a chanson, a romance, or a motet; these quotations are identified and their concordances are located, with no presumption as to their relative chronology. For motets, this also includes the liturgical chant borrowed as tenor, as well as the genre, incipit, liturgical occasion, and biblical references of the text of the chant source.

PREVIOUS EDITIONS
Principal previous editions are listed in chronological order (the first and last are always entered, whether principal or not). The presence of music is indicated by two notes (♫). Translations into modern French, English, and Italian are indicated in parentheses.

VERSIFICATION AND MUSICO-POETIC FORM

We provide versification data for each song and motet. Within our versification schemes, we add parenthetical data (joined by a plus sign) to display internal rhymes. Instances of wholly internal homophony, independent of line-end rhyme, are not noted. We understand an internal rhyme to be the result of a deliberate, purposive choice on the part of the poet. Evidence for it may be musical, syntactic, semantic, rhyme patterning, or any combination thereof. In the absence of any reason to believe in an authorial intention, we regard an apparent internal rhyme as fortuitous, a mere homophonic coincidence; we do not report such cases. Prime signs represent feminine rhymes. We place parentheses around the prime sign whenever the final -e is not sounded due to the lack of a corresponding pitch in the music. An unpaired rhyme word—that is, a line-ending word that has no rhyming partner—is designated by an x for the first such occurrence, a y for the second instance, and so forth (starting near the end of the alphabet, as needed). Lowercase italics indicate quotations. Uppercase italics indicate refrains. Musico-poetic form is given for songs only. We have adopted Dante's conventional terminology and classification. For definitions of such poetic devices as *rime brisée*, *rime dérivée*, *rime léonine*, and the like, we refer the reader to Mölk and Wolfzettel 1972, 25–27.

REFRAINS

We list all refrains and quotations catalogued in van den Boogaard 1969, regardless of whether quotations have known concordances. We use the word "refrain" to refer to lines that are positioned at the end of stanzas either in a *chanson avec des refrains* (e.g., no. 7a) or a *chanson à refrain* (e.g., no. 3a). Whenever a refrain appearing at the end of a stanza is a quotation (e.g., no. 4a), the refrain also appears, along with the location of its concordance(s), under the heading "Material." A refrain identified in a song is automatically conveyed to the corresponding motet version.

REJECTED TEXTUAL READINGS

See "Editorial Policy for the Texts and Translations."

TEXTUAL VARIANTS

See "Editorial Policy for the Texts and Translations."

NOTES TO THE MUSICAL TRANSCRIPTION

We offer an account of all our editorial interventions, covering both errors and omissions in the source, and the manner and material used to reconstruct the faulty passage. For the edition of the songs, notes are keyed to the music edition by phrase number, underlaid text, and item within the phrase (e.g., IV on "voloir," ligature bridging e′ and d′ removed). For the edition of the motets, notes are keyed to the musical transcription by part name, perfection number, underlaid text, and item within the perfection (e.g., *Motetus*. Perf. 16 e′ on "cele"). Note that in the songs, the text used to identify the passage is only that of stanza 1, even if the correction remains valid in additional stanzas. Pitches are labeled using the system in which c′ equals middle C. Other musical signs are identified as follows: a ligature bridging two pitches is signaled by a hyphen (e.g., d′-c′); three or more pitches notated as *currentes* are separated by a comma (e.g., a,g,f); a *plica* is separated from its host note by a slash (e.g., a/f). When a passage is emended through recourse to a concordance, the emendation may be either "as in" this other source (that is, the faulty passage is corrected exactly as in the concordant source) or "after" this other source (that is, the faulty matter is corrected with the help of the concordance, though adapted to the reading of the base manuscript).

MUSICAL VARIANTS

We enumerate readings from other sources that differ from our base manuscript. In the interest of concision and clarity, discrepancies regarding the presence or absence of a *tractus* in other sources are not noted. Likewise, an accidental occurring in another source that does not affect the melody is not listed. Variant readings from motet sources are not listed within the song variants and vice versa; they may be seen in the transcription and "Musical Variants" of their corresponding song or motet. For both songs and motets, variants are keyed to the musical transcription in the same manner as in the "Notes to the Musical Transcription."

COMMENTARY

Under this heading, we provide glosses and clarifications, and we discuss difficulties encountered during the editorial process; we also remark on any noteworthy aspects of the piece, such as paleographic and notational peculiarities, salient compositional features, attributions, and so forth.

TABLE I Distribution of the song corpus in trouvère manuscripts

Song	X	C	F	H	K	M	N	O	P	R	T	U	a	
1	133ᵛ–134ʳ	30ᵛ			188		89ᵛ–90ʳ		71ᵛ–72ʳ			33ᵛ–34ʳ		Bien s'est Amors bonie
2	134ʳ–ᵛ	215ʳ–ᵛ			188–189		90ʳ–ᵛ		113ʳ–ᵛ					Plaindre m'estuet de la bele en chantant
3	134ᵛ–135ʳ	113ʳ	115ʳ–116ʳ	223ᵛ	189–190	175ᵛ	90ᵛ–91ʳ	115ᵛ–116ᵛ	72ʳ–ᵛ	28ʳ–ᵛ		37ʳ	102ᵛ	Qui bien veut Amors descrivre
4a	135ʳ–ᵛ				190–191		91ʳ		72ᵛ–73ʳ	152ᵛ–153ʳ				Quant voi le douz tens venir
5a	189ᵛ–190ʳ													L'autrier de jouste un rivage
6	190ʳ				401								(124)	Touse de vile champestre
7a	190ʳ–ᵛ													Quant fueillissent li buison
8a	190ᵛ–191ʳ													Main s'est levee Aëliz
9						175ᵛ–176ʳ					153ʳ	32ʳ–ᵛ		Ja mais, por tant con l'ame el cors me bate

TABLE 2 Distribution of the polyphonic corpus in the sources

Motet	Cl	F	Mo	MüA	N	R	W_2	
4b	382ᵛ	158ᵛ	167ᵛ–168ʳ 203ᵛ–204ʳ				245ʳ⁻ᵛ	*Qant voi le douz tens venir*
5b		156ʳ					189ᵛ–190ʳ	*L'autrier de jouste un rivage*
7b			244ᵛ–245ʳ					*Quant florissent li buisson*
8b				A, 7ʳ	184ᵛ	206ⁱ		*Main s'est levee Aëlis*

TABLE 3A Strophic structure: Meter and rhyme
Sequential data (without indication of internal rhymes)

Line	1	2	3	4	5	6	7	8	9	10	11	12	13	14	15
Song | Motet															
1	6a'	6b	6a'	6b	6b	6a'	6a'	6b							
2	10a	10b'	10a	10b'	10a	10a	10b'								
3	7a'	7b'	7a'	7b'	7a'	7b'	7a'	7b'	7C	7C					
4a/1	7a	5b'	5a	7a	5b'	5a	1a	7a	1a	7a	3a	7c	4a	7a	6c
4a/2	7a	5b'	5a	7a	5b'	5a	1x	7a	1y	7a	3a	4c	7a	7a	6c
4a/3	7a	5b'	5a	7a	5b'	5a	1a	7a	1a	7a	3a	7c	4a	7a	6c
4b	7a	5b'	5a	7a	5b'	5a	1a	7a	1a	7a	3a	7x	4a	7a	6y
5a/1	7a'	7b	7a'	7b	7b	7a'	5b	7x	6b	7y	6b	7b	8b	7c	6b
5a/2	7a	8b	7a	8b	7a	7a	6b	7a	6b	7a	6b	7b	8a	7c	8a
5a/3	7a	8b	7a	8b	7a	7a	6b	7a	6b	7a	6b	7a	8b	7c	6b
5b	7a'	7b	7a'	7b	7b	7a'	5b	7x	6b	7y	6b	7b	8b	7z	6b
6	7a'	1a'	5b	2b	7a'	1a'	5c	3c	7b	2b	5d	3d	7b		
7a/1	7a	7b	7a	10b	7a	9b	10a	8b	7a	5b	7a	7c	6x	6c	
7a/2	7a	7b	7a	10b	7b	9b	10a	8b	7b	5a	7c	7c	6a*	6c●	
7b	7a	7b	7a	10b	7a	9b	10a	8b	7a	5b	7a	7c	6x	6c	
8a/1	7a	7a	7b'	5b'	5a	7a	5a	7a	7c'	4c	7c'	7c	7b		
8a/2	7a	7a	7b'	5b'	5a	7a	...	7a	7b'	4a	7b'	6a			
8b	7a	7a	7b'	5b'	5a	7a	5a	7a	7c(')	4c	7c'	7c			
9	10a'	10b'	10a'	10b'	10a'	10b'	10a'								

TABLE 3B   Strophic structure: Meter and rhyme
Sorted (without indication of internal rhymes)

Line	1	2	3	4	5	6	7	8	9	10	11	12	13	14	15
Song | Motet															
1	6a'	6b	6a'	6b	6b	6a'	6a'	6b							
4a/1	7a	5b'	5a	7a	5b'	5a	1a	7a	1a	7a	3a	7c	4a	7a	6c
4a/2	7a	5b'	5a	7a	5b'	5a	1x	7a	1y	7a	3a	4c	7a	7a	6c
4a/3	7a	5b'	5a	7a	5b'	5a	1a	7a	1a	7a	3a	7c	4a	7a	6c
4b	7a	5b'	5a	7a	5b'	5a	1a	7a	1a	7a	3a	7x	4a	7a	6y
5a/2	7a	8b	7a	8b	7b	7a	6b	7a	6b	7a	6b	7b	8a	7c	8a
5a/3	7a	8b	7a	8b	7a	7a	6b	7a	6b	7a	6b	7a	8b	7c	6b
7a/1	7a	7b	7a	10b	7a	9b	10a	8b	7a	5b	7a	7c	6x	6c	6b
7a/2	7a	7b	7a	10b	7b	9b	10a	8b	7b	5a	7c	7c	6a*	6c•	
7b	7a	7b	7a	10b	7a	9b	10a	8b	7a	5b	7a	7c	6x	6c	
8a/1	7a	7a	7b'	5b'	5a	7a	5a	7a	7c'	4c	7c'	7c	6c	6c	
8a/2	7a	7a	7b'	5b'	5a	7a	…	7a	7b'	4a	7b'	6a			
8b	7a	7a	7b'	5b'	5a	7a	5a	7a	7c(')	4c	7c(')	7c			
3	7a'	7b'	7a'	7b'	7a'	7b'	7a'	7b'	7C	7C					
5a/1	7a'	7b	7a'	7b	7b	7a'	5b	7x	6b	7y	6b	7b	8b	7c	6b
5b	7a'	7b	7a'	7b	7b	7a'	5b	7x	6b	7y	6b	7b	8b	7z	6b
6	7a'	1a'	5b	2b	7a'	1a'	5c	3c	7b	2b	5d	3d	7b		
2	10a	10b'	10a	10b'	10a	10a	10b'								
9	10a'	10b'	10a'	10b'	10a'	10b'	10a'								

TABLE 3C Inventory of rhyme types
(Stanza numbers indicated in parentheses)

1	*annexée* (2/3)					*léonine* (2)	*paronyme* (1)	
2	*annexée* (1, 1/2)	*dérivée* (1–3)	*équivoque* (1)	*homonyme* (4)	*identique* (4)	*léonine* (1–5)		*riche* (1–5)
3	*dérivée* (3)					*léonine* (1, 3)	*paronyme* (2)	*riche* (1–3, 5)
4	*dérivée* (1, 3)	*en écho* (1, 3)		*homonyme* (3)	*identique* (1–2)	*léonine* (1–3)	*paronyme* (1)	*riche* (1–3)
5	*annexée* (3)	*dérivée* (1–2)			*identique* (1–3)	*léonine* (1–2)	*paronyme* (3)	*riche* (1–3)
6			*en écho* (1–3)			*léonine* (1–3)	*paronyme* (1–3)	*riche* (1–3)
7	*dérivée* (1)					*léonine* (1–2)	*paronyme* (1–3)	*riche* (1–2)
8	*batelée* (1)					*léonine* (1–2)		*riche* (1)
9	*dérivée* (1)						*paronyme* (3)	

TABLE 4 Concordance of song and motet numbers

	Song/Motet	Raynaud-Spanke	Ludwig	Mölk-Wolfzettel	van den Boogaard	Linker	Mann
1	*Bien s'est Amors honie*	1163, 1215, 1217		860,124 [1123]		231-2	7
2	*Plaindre m'estuet de la bele en chantant*	319, 320		626,5 [598]		231-6	8
3	*Qui bien veut Amors descrivre*	1655		752,18 [837]	710	231-9	9
4a	*Quant voi le douz tens venir*	1485		576,1 [575]	1149/1580	231-8	6
4b	*Qant voi le douz tens venir*		235			265-637	
5a	*L'autrier de jouste un rivage*	35, 44a		937,1 [1442]	1424	231-4	3
5b	*L'autrier de jouste un rivage*		133a				
6	*Touse de vile champestre*	957		400,1 [514]		231-1	2
7a	*Quant fueillissent li buison*	1852		714,1 [789]	670/1242	231-7	4
7b	*Quant florissent li buisson*		137				
8a	*Main s'est levee Aeliz*	1510		384,1 [509]	689	231-5	1
8b	*Main s'est levee Aelis*		252, 565a				
9	*Ja mais, por tant con l'ame el cors me bate*	383		674,10 [703]		231-3	5

Notes

1. For full bibliographical data, see Linker 1979, no. 231.

2. See Doss-Quinby et al. 2010 for a detailed study of this genre.

3. The identification of the trouvère Robert de Reims with the author, also surnamed "La Chievre," of a (now lost) romance of Tristan cited in the *Roman de Renart*, held as plausible by Mann (1898), has long since been dismissed; see Jeanroy 1899.

4. We are grateful to Robert Lug for having shared with us his as-yet-unpublished findings on manuscript *U*. Some of his conclusions are already available in Lug 2000 and 2012.

5. In manuscript *a*, the incipit *Touse de vile champestre* is indexed to fol. 124 (in the contemporaneous foliation); this folio is now missing (see Commentary on song no. 6).

6. Chansonnier *O* was copied around 1300; in parts of the songbook, the notation mimics the measured notation of the motet.

7. See Commentary on song no. 2.

8. See Commentary on songs nos. 1 and 3.

9. On the dating of trouvère songbooks, see Aubrey 2001.

10. W_2 can be dated to the mid-thirteenth century (Everist 1989, 97–110). It is somewhat difficult to date *MüA* owing to its very fragmentary condition, but its notation and contents are comparable to those of W_2.

11. Brakelmann suggested, as early as 1868, the grouping of trouvère chansonniers according to five distinct families, one being composed of *KNPO* (1868a, 51–55). In 1886 Schwan distinguished three main traditions, the most important being the one joining *KNPXLV* (86–173) and the one grouping the Chansonnier de Noailles and the Chansonnier du Roi with *aAZ* (19–86). Musicologists then claimed that, on account of their musical convergences, *KNPX* were probably copied from the same great anthology, unlike Noailles and Roi, whose divergences suggest they were produced from various collections (Karp 1964, 32–47; Parker 1978). These four songbooks were all very likely copied in Artois or Picardy in the 1270s or 1280s, *K* and *N* sharing the same literary hand and the same decorative style (see Aubrey 2001; Huot 1987, 46–64).

12. For a description of this and neighboring varieties of the medieval language, see, among other works, Buridant 2000. There are various works offering guidance in the pronunciation of Old French; see, for example, Rosenberg et al. 1998, 30–31.

13. Within the corpus of trouvère song, the other texts making intensive use of echo rhymes are very few in number and come later; among them, a chanson (RS 2101a) by Gilles le Vinier, whose production is situated in the second quarter of the thirteenth century, is a contrafact of RS 957 (our song no. 6), thus identifying Robert as the master of this procedure. As detailed in Saint-Cricq 2019, later songs with intensive echo rhyming include a second chanson (RS 257) by Gilles le Vinier; a chanson (RS 556) by Gautier de Coinci, found in the second part of his *Miracles*, which date to the 1220s/1230s; and a rondeau (rond. 190) copied in *k*, a chansonnier from the early fourteenth century.

14. The varied modalities of the versification of this corpus are analyzed in Rosenberg with Doss-Quinby 2016.

15. The letter following a chanson number indicates the particular manuscript version.

16. Note too that *M* and *T*, however close in contents and song texts, frequently show divergent melodies for a given song (see Karp 1964, 32–47; Parker 1978; Haines 1998, 94–96).

17. Note that *R* also retains the principle of anaphora, with a transposition of the motif from phrases I / III to II / IV.

18. See "Robert de Reims, dit La Chievre: What We Know, What We Can Surmise" above.

19. For the dating of *T*, see Saint-Cricq et al. 2017, VIII; for *X*, see Aubrey 2001; Huot 1987, 46–64.

20. This section on the motets and their attendant songs offers a brief summary of this article, with a few selected examples. The fact that Robert de Reims was most certainly the author of original motets later turned into clausulæ and then into strophic songs is exhaustively demonstrated in the article, and is here merely taken as a given.

21. On this question, see the details and examples in Saint-Cricq 2019.

22. See Huot 1997, 16, 173.

23. Some upper voices of polyphonic motets appear devoid of their tenor and without supplementary stanzas, notably within the song collections of chansonniers *M*, *T*, and *a*.

24. All these works are anthologized in Bec 1977–78, 2:150–55. On the motifs of the Aelis archetype, see Huot 1997, 57–59; Bec 1981, 250–53.

25. For a study of the monophonic motet in *N* and/or *I* and its link to the chanson, see Butterfield 2003; Peraino 2011, chap. 4; Leach 2018; Saint-Cricq 2018. For an analysis of the motets built on vernacular songs, see Everist 2007. For an account of the motets built according to the chanson's formal types, see Everist 1988; Saint-Cricq 2013.

26. For an account of the traditional view with appropriate bibliographical references, see Bradley 2018, 1–6.

27. A complete list of the works that appear both as motetus voices in motet collections and as monophonic trouvère songs in chansonniers, along with the names of the trouvères associated with them, is provided in Saint-Cricq 2019.

28. We have prepared similar policy statements for a number of earlier publications, adapting each to the challenge of the texts at hand. The interested reader can find these readily.

29. For an exhaustive overview of the rhythmic modes and the principles of discant, see Roesner 1993, lxxxv–xc.

30. Ludwig's cataloguing system and numbers appear with updates and emendations in Gennrich 1957 and Van der Werf 1989.

Songs and Motets

1   Bien s'est Amors honie   Chanson

Bien s'est Amors honie
Quant el m'a si traïs
Qu'el m'a fet sans amie
Amer, tant con sui vis.   1.4
Mort sui, ce m'est avis,
Por ce que je n'aim mie.
Ne ja més en ma vie
Ne serai fins amis.   1.8

La grant joie est faillie
Que me faisoit touz dis
Amors, par tricherie,
Qui tout m'avoit conquis.   2.4
Las! je m'estoie mis
Dou tout en sa baillie;
Or s'est de moi partie.
Ja més n'i serai pris.   2.8

Pris? Por quoi i seroie,
Quant g'en sui eschapés?
Ne sai; més tels foloie
Qui puis revient assés   3.4
La dont il est grevés.
Deus! se je ce faisoie,

Plus douce amor avroie;
Més trop m'en sui blasmés.

3.8

Tost m'en repentiroie
Se j'estoie apensés,
Par foi! que ge·l disoie
Come hons desesperés:

4.4

"Amors, si m'ociés,
Certes, car ge·l vodroie!
La force n'est pas moie,
Vers vos, bien le savés."

4.8

I

                      ❧

Love has dishonored itself
by so betraying me
that it has made me love with no one
to love, for the rest of my life.

1.4

I am dead, it seems to me,
because I live without love.
And never in my life
will I be a true lover.

1.8

Gone is the great joy
I experienced day after day
from Love, which, with deceit,
had conquered me utterly.

2.4

Alas! I had placed myself
utterly under its power—
and now it has abandoned me.
Nevermore will I be caught in its trap!

2.8

Trapped? Why again would I be,
now that I've made my way out?
I don't know; but a man is a fool
if he hurries back to a place

3.4

where he is tortured.
God! If I did that,
I would have a sweeter love,
but I have blamed myself too readily.   3.8

I would soon have regrets
if I were inclined—
my goodness!—to say,
like a man without hope: 4.4
"Love, come kill me,
for I would truly like you to!
I don't have the strength [it would take],
unlike you, as you well know."   4.8

I   ❧

Amour s'est bien déshonorée
quand elle m'a tant trahi
que, sans que j'aie même d'amie, elle m'a contraint
à aimer pour le restant de ma vie.   1.4
Je suis mort, me semble-t-il,
parce que je n'aime point.
Et jamais de ma vie
je ne serai un fin amant.   1.8

La grande joie n'est plus
que m'apportait à tout moment,
par tricherie, Amour,
qui m'avait entièrement conquis.   2.4
Hélas! je m'étais soumis
entièrement à son pouvoir;
or, voilà qu'elle m'a abandonné!
Plus jamais je n'y serai piégé!   2.8

Piégé? Pourquoi le serais-je,
ayant enfin échappé à son emprise?

Je ne sais, mais il est fou,
celui qui persiste à revenir 3.4
là où il a été maltraité.
Dieu! si j'agissais de la sorte,
je connaîtrais une amour plus douce;
mais je m'en suis déjà trop blâmé. 3.8

Je m'en repentirais assez vite,
si j'étais enclin—
mon Dieu!—à m'exprimer
en homme désespéré: 4.4
"Amour, tuez-moi donc;
c'est en effet ce que je voudrais!
Je n'en ai pas la force,
contrairement à vous, vous le savez bien!" 4.8

I

Bien s'est A - mors ho - ni - - e
La grant joie est fail - li - - e
Pris? Por quoi i se - roi - - e,
Tost m'en re - pen - ti - roi - - e

II

Quant el m'a si tra - - is
Que me fai - soit touz dis
Quant g'en sui es - cha - pés?
Se j'es - toie a - pen - sés,

III

Qu'el m'a fet sans a - mi - e
A - mors, par tri - che - ri - e,
Ne sai; més tels fo - loi - e
Par foi! que ge·l di - soi - e

IV

A - mer, tant con sui vis.
Qui tout m'a - voit con - quis.
Qui puis re - vient as - sés
Come hons de - ses - pe - rés:

V

Mort sui, ce m'est a - - vis,
Las! je m'es - toi - e mis
La dont il est gre - - vés.
"A - mors, si m'o - ci - - és,

VI

Por ce que je n'aim mi - - e.
Dou tout en sa bail - li - - e;
Deus! se je ce fai - soi - - e,
Cer - tes, car ge·l vo - droi - - e!

VII

Ne ja - més en ma vi - - e
Or s'est de moi par - ti - - e.
Plus douce a - mor a - vroi - - e;
La for - ce n'est pas moi - - e,

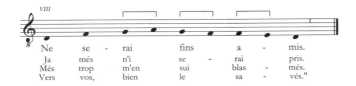

VIII

Ne	se	rai		fins	a		mis.
Ja	més	n'i		se	rai		pris.
Més	trop	m'en		sui	blas		més.
Vers	vos,	bien		le	sa		vés."

CATALOGUING
Raynaud-Spanke 1163, 1215, 1217; Linker 231-2; Mölk-Wolfzettel 860,124 [1123]

MANUSCRIPTS
X 133ᵛ–134ʳ ♫ (*robert de rains*), *C* 30ᵛ (*Blondelz*), *K* 188 ♫ (*la chievre de rains*), *N* 89ᵛ–90ʳ ♫ (*Robert de rains*), *P* 71ᵛ–72ʳ ♫ (*Robert de rains*), *U* 33ᵛ–34ʳ (empty staves)

PREVIOUS EDITIONS
Tarbé 1850, 101; Tarbé 1862, 15; Hofmann 1867, 492; Brakelmann 1868b, 241; Mann 1898, 28; Mann 1899, 106; Lachèvre and Guégan 1914, 3ʳ; Lachèvre et al. 1917, 27, 49 ♫ (French translation); Jeanroy and Långfors 1921, 27; Lepage 1994, 365; Bahat and Le Vot 1996, 89 ♫ ; Tischler 1997, 8: no. 664 ♫ ; Tyssens 2015, 1:140

VERSIFICATION AND MUSICO-POETIC FORM
4, *coblas doblas* in *oda continua*; *rime annexée* (2/3), *rime léonine* (2), *rime paronyme* (1)

	1	2	3	4	5	6	7	8
	6a′	6b	6a′	6b	6b	6a′	6a′	6b
	1/2	3/4						
a′	ie	oie						
b	is	és						

REJECTED TEXTUAL READINGS
1.3 Qu'el m'a fet *missing (–3) (reading from KNP)* — 2.5 mis *missing (–1) (reading from CKNPU)* — 3.6 Deus] dex — 4.2 ie estoie *(+1) (reading from CKNPU)* — 4.4 home *(+1) (reading from KNP)*

TEXTUAL VARIANTS
1.1 s'est] cest *C*; amors *followed by expunctuated* trai *P*; honie] trichie *C*, traie *U* — 1.2 elle mait ocis *CU* — 1.3 Qu'el] ki *CU* — 1.5 mors *CKU*; ce] se *C* — 2.1 granz *U*; La ioie mest f. *C* — 2.2 Ke mait faite *C*, Qui ma fointe *U* — 2.3 par sa t. *N* — 2.4 Ke tout

auoit *C* — 2.5 mestoie *followed by expunctuated* tot *P* — 2.7 s'est] cest *C* — 2.8 James *copied twice in N, with second iteration expunctuated*; n'i] ne *C*; ni serai iamais pris *U* — 3.1 Pris ie por coy s. *C*; Ge por qoi pris s. *U* — 3.2 g'en] ie *C* — 3.3 tels] teil *CNP*; foloie] folie *C*, *missing N* — 3.4 Qui] ke *C* — 3.7 douce amor] douce mort *C*, dolce-mant *U* — 4.1 Tost] tot *P*, ie *CU*; m'en] me *U* — 4.2 apensés] apassez *N*, eschaipeis *CU* — 4.3 ie parloie *CU* — 4.4 Com hom *CU* — 4.5 si] sei *with expunctuated* e *P*, cor *C*, car *U* — 4.6 car ge·l] ie le *CU*

Manuscripts *CU* record two additional stanzas (presented here based on *U*):

Dame, si dolz martire
Doi je bien endurer,
Ne jamais Nostre Sire
Ne·l me puisse amender   5.4
Se ja m'en quier oster!
Se me volez ocire,
Je ne sai pas eslire
Meillor mort, ne trover.   5.8

D'Amors ne sai que dire:
Qant plus i voil panser,
Une hore me fait rire,
L'autre me fait plorer.   6.4
Ja ne l'en doi blasmer,
Mais maltalenz et ire
Me fait dire et desdire
Et folement parler.   6.8

Lady, I must indeed endure
such sweet martyrdom,
and may Our Lord never
let me make amends   5.4
if I ever seek to free myself of it!
If you want to kill me,
I can't think of choosing—
or finding—a better death.   5.8

I don't know what to say about Love:
the more I try to think about it,

[the more I find that] one moment it makes me laugh
[and] the next it makes me cry.   6.4
I mustn't ever blame [Love] for this,
but ill will and anger
make me say one thing, then another,
and speak like a fool.   6.8

Dame, je dois bien endurer
un si doux martyre—
que Notre Seigneur
ne me le pardonne aucunement   5.4
si je cherchais jamais à m'en libérer!
Si vous voulez me tuer,
je ne saurais choisir,
ni trouver, meilleure mort.   5.8

Je ne sais que dire d'Amour:
plus j'y pense,
[plus je trouve que] tantôt elle me fait rire,
tantôt elle me fait pleurer.   6.4
Je ne dois jamais l'en blâmer,
mais le dépit et la colère
me font dire des choses contradictoires
et parler comme un fou.   6.8

Versification

	1	2	3	4	5	6	7	8
	6a′	6b	6a′	6b	6b	6a′	6a′	6b
a′	ire							
b	er							

Textual Variants

   5.1 si] cest *C* — 5.4 Ne·l] ne *C* — 5.5 ja] ie *C* — 5.6 me deuies *C* — 5.7 sai] puis *C*
   — 6.2 plus] muels *C* — 6.3 Lune h. *C* — 6.5 ne men doit *C* — 6.6 malz talens *C*

III first three pitches added in the margin without text — III *tractus* added after last pitch as at the other phrase closures — V *tractus* added after last pitch as in *K* — VII *tractus* added after last pitch as in *N* — VIII triple *tractus* signaling end of stanza after last pitch and syllable

MUSICAL VARIANTS

I a unplicated ("ni-") *KNP* — VI c/b ("n'aim") *KNP* — VII a ("ma") *K* — IX c ("ne") *N*

COMMENTARY

This composition opens the first group of songs by Robert in manuscript *X*; it appears under the rubric "Ci comencent les chançons robert de rains." In manuscript *C*, whose rubrics are "généralement de peu de valeur" (Lepage 1994, 371), this song is ascribed to Blondel de Nesle. In manuscripts *KNPX,* this song is always first within a group of three (*P*) or four (*KNX*) songs ascribed to Robert de Reims (see table 1). Consequently, in his edition of Blondel de Nesle, Lepage characterizes the attribution to Blondel in *C* as "douteuse." — 1.5, V Declensional variation in manuscript *X*, especially with *mor-* and *amor-*, is sufficiently frequent to lead us to conclude that the apparently erroneous form *mort* probably stems from early case-system deterioration. For that reason, we have opted to respect this manuscript reading rather than introduce a correction. See also song no. 4a, line 3.14, XI.

2 Plaindre m'estuet de la bele en chantant

Chanson

Plaindre m'estuet de la bele en chantant,
Tant seulement qu'ele oie la nouvele,
Coment s'amor vet mon cuer enchantant,
Que tout adés ses maus li renovele,
N'onques d'amer ne se va repentant.   1.5
Més ce me vient touz jors bien a creant
De li servir: s'iert m'atente plus bele.

Belement va son secors atendant,
Qui de douz cuer et vrai merci apele.
Et li miens cuers i va touz jors tendant
C'onques vers li ne trest fausse merelle.
Més or me vois tres bien aparcevant: 2.5
S'ensi me vait longuement decevant,
Li premiers maus a gregnor me rapele.

Si sachiés bien, dame, tout vraiement,
Qu'or est mestiers que j'aie vostre aïe,
Que ja sans vos, por nul rapaiement,
N'iert de mon cors la dolor rapaïe.
Je ne·l di pas por nul retraiement,   3.5
Qu'assés vaut melz la mort en paiement,
Que bone amor soit por moi delaïe.

Més c'est, espoir, d'aucun essaiement,
De quoi Amors me fait tele envaïe.
Et je la serf sanz nul essaiement;
Si sai de voir que bien en iert païe
Ma volenté; car de tel paiement   4.5
Sont cil paié qui sans delaiement
Ont bone amor de fin cuer essaïe.

Douce dame, plaine de grant bonté,
La cui biauté nus ne savroit descrire,
Bien avroie tout autre sormonté,
Se me daigniés a vostre ami eslire;
Car tant vos aim! Ja n'estoit raconté   5.5

Li maus que sent, et si sui si donté,
C'onques n'osai vostre voloir desdire.

2

I must complain of my lady in song,
until she understands
how my love for her holds my heart in thrall,
for at every moment [my heart] feels its pain anew,
yet never does it have misgivings;   1.5
indeed, I always find it a pleasure
to serve her; that way my wait will be lighter.

Lightly does a man await satisfaction,
when he appeals for mercy with a kind and true heart;
and my heart always strives toward that end,
[this heart,] which has never treated her unfairly;
but now, as I am ever more aware,   2.5
if she long continues to thwart me,
the initial pain leads me to one greater.

So realize, lady, in all truth,
that I am now in need of your aid,
for never without you, despite any blunting,
will the pain in my body be [sufficiently] blunted;
I say this with no reservation at all,   3.5
for it is much better to pay the price of death
than to endure the delay of good love.

But it is, I suppose, for some sort of test
that Love invades me this way.
Yet I serve [my lady] with no hesitation;
indeed, I know truly that my desire
will be satisfied, for such satisfaction   4.5
rewards those who, without wavering,
have aspired to good love with a true heart.

Dear lady, full of great goodness,
whose beauty no one could describe,
I would readily surpass anyone
if you deigned to choose me as your lover,
for I love you so much! No one has ever recounted   5.5
such love as I feel, and I am so overcome
that I have never dared oppose your command.

2   ॐ

Il faut que je me plaigne de la belle en chantant,
jusqu'à ce qu'elle se rende compte
à quel point l'amour qu'elle inspire en moi ensorcelle mon cœur,
qui a tout moment sent renaître son mal
sans jamais remettre son amour en question.   1.5
Or, cela me fait toujours grand plaisir
de la servir; ainsi mon attente en sera plus légère.

Agréablement, c'est ainsi qu'attend son secours
celui qui en fait la demande d'un cœur doux et sincère;
et mon cœur avance toujours vers ce but,
car jamais il ne s'est montré déloyal à son égard.
Mais maintenant j'ai fort bien conscience que,   2.5
si elle me déjoue ainsi continûment,
le premier mal ne me mènera que vers un pire encore.

Sachez donc bien, dame, en vérité,
qu'il est grand temps que je reçoive votre aide,
car sans vous, en dépit de tout autre apaisement,
la douleur de mon corps ne sera jamais apaisée.
Je dis cela sans aucune réserve,   3.5
car il vaut bien mieux payer le prix en mourant
que faire obstacle à bonne amour.

Mais c'est, je crois, pour me mettre à épreuve
qu'Amour m'envahit ainsi.
Je la sers, sans [redouter] aucune épreuve;
et je sais, à vrai dire, que mon désir sera exaucé,
car de cette sorte de récompense   4.5
sont récompensés ceux qui, sans hésitation,
ont d'un cœur loyal subi l'épreuve de bonne amour.

Douce dame, pleine de grande bonté,
dont nul ne saurait décrire la beauté,
j'aurais vite surpassé tout homme
si vous daigniez me choisir comme amant,
car je vous aime tant! Nul n'a jamais décrit   5.5
les peines que je sens, et pourtant je suis dompté,
au point que je n'ai jamais osé m'opposer à votre volonté.

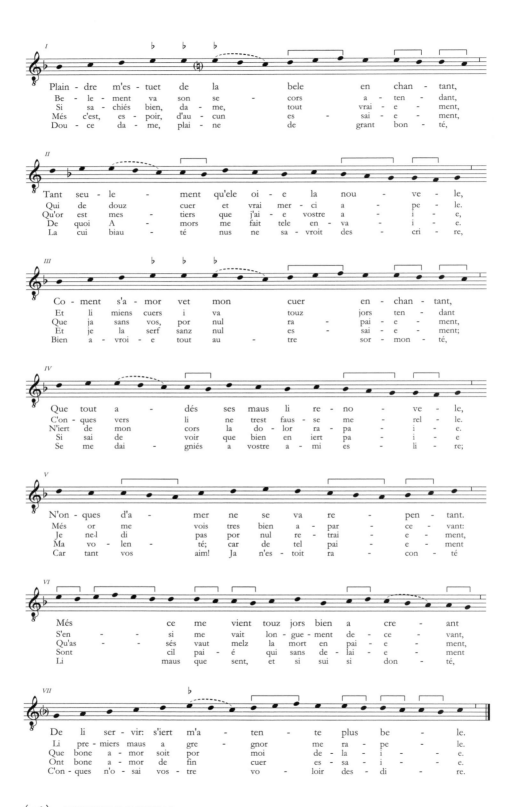

I

Plain - dre m'es - tuet de la bele en chan - tant,
Be - le - ment va son se - cors a - ten - dant,
Si sa - chiés bien, da - me, tout vrai - e - ment,
Més c'est, es - poir, d'au - cun es - sai - e - ment,
Dou - ce da - me, plai - ne de grant bon - té,

II

Tant seu - le - ment qu'ele oi - e la nou - ve - le,
Qui de douz cuer et vrai mer - ci a - pe - le.
Qu'or est mes - tiers que j'ai - e vostre a - i - e,
De quoi A - mors me fait tele en - va - i - e.
La cui biau - té nus ne sa - vroit des - cri - re,

III

Co - ment s'a - mor vet mon cuer en - chan - tant,
Et li miens cuers i va touz jors ten - dant,
Et je la serf sanz nul es - sai - e - ment;
Bien a - vroi - e tout au - tre sor - mon - té,

IV

Que tout a - dés ses maus li re - no - ve - le,
C'on - ques vers li ne trest faus - se me - rel - le.
N'iert de mon cors la do - lor ra - pa - i - e.
Si sai de voir que bien en iert pa - i - e
Se me dai - gniés a vostre a - mi es - li - re;

V

N'on - ques d'a - mer ne se va re - pen - tant.
Més or me vois tres bien a - par - ce - vant:
Je ne·l di pas por nul re - trai - e - ment,
Ma vo - len - té; car de tel pai - e - ment
Car tant vos aim! Ja n'es - toit ra - con - té

VI

Més ce me vient touz jors bien a cre - ant
S'en - - si me vait lon - gue - ment de - ce - vant,
Qu'as - - sés vaut melz la mort en pai - e - ment,
Sont cil pai - é qui sans de - lai - e - ment
Li maus que sent, et si sui si don - té,

VII

De li ser - vir: s'iert m'a - ten - te plus be - le.
Li pre - miers maus a gre - gnor me ra - pe - le.
Que bone a - mor soit por moi de - la - i - e.
Ont bone a - mor de fin cuer es - sa - i - e.
C'on - ques n'o - sai vos - tre vo - loir des - di - re.

CATALOGUING

Raynaud-Spanke 319, 320; Linker 231-6; Mölk-Wolfzettel 626,5 [598]

MANUSCRIPTS

X 134$^{\mathrm{r-v}}$ ♪ (*Robert de rains*), *C* 215$^{\mathrm{r-v}}$, *K* 188–189 ♪ (*la chevre de rains*), *N* 90$^{\mathrm{r-v}}$ ♪ , *P* 113$^{\mathrm{r-v}}$ ♪ (*la chievre de rains*)

PREVIOUS EDITIONS

Wackernagel 1846, 48; Tarbé 1850, 64; Mann 1898, 26; Mann 1899, 104; Lachèvre and Guégan 1914, 4^{v}; Lachèvre et al. 1917, 28, 50 ♪ (French translation); Tischler 1997, 3: no. 190 ♪

VERSIFICATION AND MUSICO-POETIC FORM

5, *coblas doblas* in *pedes cum cauda*; *rime annexée* (1, 1/2), *rime dérivée* (1–3), *rime équivoque* (1), *rime homonyme* (4), *rime identique* (4), *rime léonine* (1–5), *rime riche* (1–5)

1	2	3	4	5	6	7
10a	10b´	10a	10b´	10a	10a	10b´

	1/2	3/4	5
a	ant	aiement	onté
b´	el(l)e	aïe	ire

REJECTED TEXTUAL READINGS

1.2 enquele *(+1) (reading from CKNP)* — 2.2 uerai *(+1) (reading from CKNP)* — 2.6 missing *(reading from C)* — 2.7 qui a *(reading from P)*; mapele *(reading from CP)* — 3.4 rapaiee *(reading from NP)* — 3.6 lamor *(reading from C)* — 3.7 delaiee *(reading from NP)* — 4.3 engingnement *(reading from CKNP)* — 4.4 paiee — 5.6 donté] doutes *(reading from C)* — 5.7 voloir] uolente *(+1) (reading from CKN)*

TEXTUAL VARIANTS

1.1 Renoueleir ueul la *C* — 1.4 ses] ces *C* — 1.5 N'onques] onkes *C* — 1.6 Aincois li uient *C* — 1.7 s'iert] ciert *C*; mentente *CN* — 2.2 cuer *missing N* — 2.3 c. uait *C*; atandant *C* — 2.4 Nonkes *C* — 2.5 me] men *C*; tres] moult *C* — 2.6 *missing in KNP* — 2.7 ou gringnors *C*, que (qui *N*) a greigneur *KN*; mapele *KN* — 3.1 Si] se *C*; ueraiement *N* — 3.2 mestier *P* — 3.4 d. repairie *C*, rapaiee *K* — 3.5 Je] ne *C* — 3.6 Caincois ain muels *C*; lamor *KNP* — 3.7 essaie *C*, delaiee *K* — 4.2 De quo *N*; Kire damors mait fait *C*; tele enuaiee *K* — 4.4 Si] se *C*; en] men *C*; paiee *CKNP* — 4.6 Soncil *N*; ki en teil essiant *C* — 4.7 On bone a. et de *C*; essaiee *KNP* — 5.1 dame tous sens toute bonteis *C* — 5.2 cui] qui *KNP*; ne porroit *N* — 5.3 aueroie tous autres *C* — 5.4 me] moi *C*

— 5.5 nestroit rescontei *C* — 5.6 Le mal *P*; kensant et sen seux *C*; doutez *KP*, dontez *N* — 5.7 *missing in P*

Manuscripts *CP* record a sixth stanza (presented here based on *P*):
Bien i doit estre en guerredon contez
Li bons travaus, qui tot mon cors enpire;
Més de haut cuer descent haute bontez,
Por ce m'atent que vos m'i soiés mire.
Et se mes cuers est en haut lieu montez,   6.5
Par Amors s'est maint bas hons amontez;
Qui plus haut tent, de greignor joie est sire.

One can certainly take as a reward
the good torment that afflicts my whole body;
but from a noble heart derives noble goodness,
wherefore I expect you to be my healer.
And if my heart aspires to a noble height,   6.5
[it's because] many a lowly man has risen through Love;
the higher a man's aims, the greater his joy.

Le bon tourment qui afflige tout mon corps
doit être considéré comme une récompense;
mais d'un cœur noble provient une noble bonté,
d'où mon espoir que vous me guérissiez.
Et si mon cœur cherche à s'ennoblir,   6.5
[c'est qu'] Amour a élevé maint homme humble;
plus on aspire haut, plus la joie que l'on atteint est grande.

Versification

	1	2	3	4	5	6	7
	10a	10b´	10a	10b´	10a	10a	10b´
a	ontez						
b´	ire						

Rejected Textual Readings
   6.1 conte

6.1 i] me; a g. tornez *C* — 6.2 lons t. ke *C* — 6.4 ke ma dame en soit *C* — 6.6 a. est mains haus hom esmonteis *C*

NOTES TO THE MUSICAL TRANSCRIPTION

I on "bele", extra e′ appears after d′-e′-f′ due to voicing of "-le": emended as in *KNP* — II on "-ment", extra d′ appears after c′-b due to setting of extra word "en": emended as in *KNP* — III *tractus* added after last pitch as in I — IV c′ on "que": emended as in I and *KNP* — VI *tractus* added after last pitch as in *K* — VII triple *tractus* signaling end of stanza after last pitch and syllable

MUSICAL VARIANTS

VI c′ ("a") *P*

COMMENTARY

This is the second song in a group of four consecutive compositions by Robert copied in manuscript *N*. In an apparent oversight, the rubricator indicates Robert's name at the start of each song except this one.

Qui bien veut Amors descrivre,
Amors est et male et bone;
Le plus mesurable enyvre
Et le plus sage enbricone;
Les enprisonés delivre,   1.5
Les delivrés enprisone;
Chascun fait morir et vivre,
Et a chascun tout et done.
Et fole et sage est Amors,
Vie, mors, joie et dolours.   1.10

Amors est large et avere,
C'est qui le voir en retraie.
Amors est douce et amere
A celui qui bien l'essaie.
Amors est marrastre et mere,   2.5
Primes bat et puis rapaie;
Et cil qui plus le conpere,
C'est cil qui mains s'en esmaie.
[Et fole et sage est Amors,
Vie, mors, joie et dolours.]   2.10

Amors va par aventure:
Chascuns i pert et gaaigne.
Par outrage et par mesure
Sane chascun et mahaigne.
Eürs et Mesaventure   3.5
Sont touz jors en sa conpaigne.
Por c'est raisons et droiture
Que chascuns s'en lot et plaigne.
[Et fole et sage est Amors,
Vie, mors, joie et dolours.]   3.10

Souvent rit et souvent pleure
Qui bien aime en son corage.
Bien et mal li queurent seure,
Son preu quiert et son damage.

Et se li biens li demeure,   4.5
De tant a il avantage,
Que li biens d'une seule heure
Les maus d'un an assoage.
[Et fole et sage est Amors,
Vie, mors, joie et dolours.]   4.10

La Chievre dit sans faintise
D'Amors, en la definaille,
De ce que il en devise,
Qu'ensi le trueve on sans faille,
Car cil qui Amors justise   5.5
Et qui por li se travaille
Ne porroit en nule guise
Le grain cuillir sans la paille.
[Et fole et sage est Amors,
Vie, mors, joie et dolours.]   5.10

3   ❧

Here is the true description of Love:
Love is both good and bad;
it intoxicates the most sensible man
and confounds the most wise;
it frees men imprisoned   1.5
and imprisons those who are freed;
to everyone it brings death and gives life,
and in every case it takes and it gives.
And Love is both foolish and wise;
[it is] life and death, joy and sadness.   1.10

Love is generous and miserly,
it depends on who's describing the experience.
Love is both bitter and sweet
for the man who tastes it with discernment.
Love is both stepmother and mother;   2.5

first it beats and then it consoles;
and the man who suffers most [for Love]
is the one who is least dismayed by it.
And Love is both foolish and wise;
it is life and death, joy and sadness.   2.10

Love is ruled by chance:
everyone loses and everyone wins.
Through excess and through moderation
it both heals and wounds everyone.
Good Luck and ill Fortune   3.5
are always [together] in its company.
That's why it is right and just
that everyone delight [in Love] and complain of it.
And Love is both foolish and wise;
it is life and death, joy and sadness.   3.10

Often laughing and often weeping
is he who feels love in his heart.
Good and bad rush in upon him;
he seeks both his profit and his loss.
And if the good is long delayed,   4.5
that's actually to his advantage,
for the good that lasts a single hour
alleviates the pains of an entire year.
And Love is both foolish and wise;
it is life and death, joy and sadness.   4.10

La Chievre states frankly,
in conclusion, about Love
[and] how he portrays it,
that this is truly how one experiences it,
for anyone who is under Love's command   5.5
and suffers its hardships
would be wholly incapable
of harvesting the grain without the straw.
And Love is both foolish and wise;
it is life and death, joy and sadness.   5.10

3

Voici comment bien décrire Amour:
elle est à la fois méchante et bonne;
elle enivre le plus mesuré
et rend fou le plus sage;
elle libère ceux qui sont captifs   1.5
et emprisonne ceux qui sont libres;
à chacun elle apporte la mort et la vie,
et à chacun elle dérobe et elle donne.
Amour est folle, Amour est sage;
elle est vie, mort, joie et douleur.   1.10

Amour est généreuse et avare,
selon qui en fait la description.
Amour est à la fois douce et amère
pour qui en a fait l'expérience.
Amour est marâtre et mère;   2.5
elle bat d'abord et ensuite console;
et celui qui en souffre le plus
est celui qui s'en inquiète le moins.
Amour est folle, Amour est sage;
elle est vie, mort, joie et douleur.   2.10

Amour est gouvernée par le hasard;
chacun y perd, chacun y gagne.
Par l'excès et par la modération
elle guérit chacun et blesse tout le monde.
Bonne Chance et mauvaise Fortune   3.5
vont de pair à ses côtés.
C'est pourquoi il est raisonnable et juste
que chacun s'y plaise et s'en plaigne.
Amour est folle, Amour est sage;
elle est vie, mort, joie et douleur.   3.10

Souvent rit et souvent pleure
celui qui sent l'amour dans son cœur.
Le bien et le mal se précipitent sur lui;
il cherche à la fois son profit et sa perte.

Et si son bonheur s'attarde,   4.5
c'est après tout un avantage,
car le bonheur d'une seule heure
adoucit la souffrance de toute une année.
Amour est folle, Amour est sage;
elle est vie, mort, joie et douleur.   4.10

La Chièvre dit sans ambages,
pour conclure, à propos d'Amour
dont il fait ici le portrait,
que c'est ainsi, sans faute, qu'on la trouve;
car celui qui est sous l'emprise d'Amour   5.5
et qui souffre à cause d'elle
ne pourrait nullement
récolter le grain sans la paille.
Amour est folle, Amour est sage;
elle est vie, mort, joie et douleur.   5.10

X, 134ᵛ-135ʳ

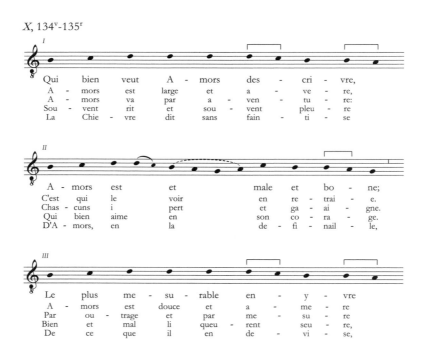

I

Qui bien veut A - mors des - cri - vre,
A - mors est large et a - ve - re,
A - mors va par a - ven - tu - re:
Sou - vent rit et sou - vent pleu - re
La Chie - vre dit sans fain - ti - se

II

A - mors est et male et bo - ne;
C'est qui le voir en re - trai - e.
Chas - cuns i pert et ga - ai - gne.
Qui bien aime en son co - ra - ge.
D'A - mors, en la de - fi - nail - le,

III

Le plus me - su - rable en - y - vre
A - mors est douce et a - me - re
Par ou - trage et par me - su - re
Bien et mal li queu - rent seu - re,
De ce que il en de - vi - se,

IV

Et le plus sage en bri - co - ne;
A ce - lui qui bien l'es - sai - e.
Sa - ne chas - cun et ma - hai - gne.
Son preu quiert et son da - ma - ge.
Qu'en - si le trueve on sans fail - le,

V

Les en - pri - so - nés de - li - vre,
A - mors est mar - rastre et me - re,
E - urs et Me - sa - ven - tu - re
Et se li biens li de - meu - re,
Car cil qui A - mors jus - ti - se

VI

Les de - li - vrés en - pri - so - ne;
Pri - mes bat et puis ra - pai - e;
Sont touz jors en sa con - pai - gne.
De tant a il a - van - ta - ge,
Et qui por li se tra - vail - le

VII

Chas - cun fait mo - rir et vi - vre,
Et cil qui plus le con - pe - re,
Por c'est rai - sons et droi - tu - re
Que li biens d'u - ne seule heu - re
Ne por - roit en nu - le gui - se

VIII

Et a chas - cun tout et do - ne.
C'est cil qui mains s'en es - mai - e.
Que chas - cuns s'en lot et plai - gne.
Les maus d'un an as - so - a - ge.
Le grain cuil - lir sans la pail - le.

refrain

IX

Et fole et sage est A - mors,

X

Vi - e, mors, joie et do - lours.

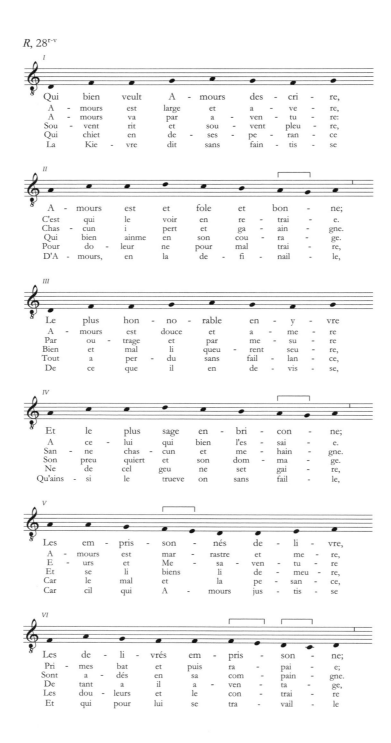

I

Qui bien veult A - mours des - cri - re,
A - mours est large et a - ve - re,
A - mours va par a - ven - tu - re:
Sou - vent rit et sou - vent pleu - re,
Qui chiet en de - ses - pe - ran - ce
La Kie - vre dit sans fain - tis - se

II

A - mours est et fole et bon - ne;
C'est qui le voir en re - trai - e.
Chas - cun i pert et ga - ain - gne.
Qui bien ainme en son cou - ra - ge.
Pour do - leur ne pour mal trai - re,
D'A - mours, en la de - fi - nail - le,

III

Le plus hon - no - rable en - y - vre
A - mours est douce et a - me - re
Par ou - trage et par me - su - re
Bien et mal li queu - rent seu - re,
Tout a per - du sans fail - lan - ce,
De ce que il en de - vis - se,

IV

Et le plus sage en - bri - con - ne;
A ce - lui qui bien l'es - sai - e.
San - ne chas - cun et me - hain - gne.
Son preu quiert et son dom - ma - ge.
Ne de cel geu ne set gai - re,
Qu'ains - si le trueve on sans fail - le,

V

Les em - pris - son - nés de - li - vre,
A - mours est mar - rastre et me - re,
E - urs et Me - sa - ven - tu - re
Et se li biens li de - meu - re,
Car le mal et la pe - san - ce,
Car cil qui A - mours jus - tis - se

VI

Les de - li - vrés em - pris - son - ne;
Pri - mes bat et puis ra - pai - e;
Sont a - dés en sa com - pain - gne.
De tant a il a - ven - ta - ge,
Les dou - leurs et le con - trai - re
Et qui pour lui se tra - vail - le

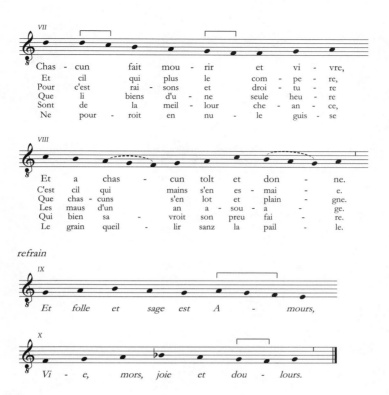

VII

Chas - cun fait mou – rir et vi – vre,
Et cil qui plus le com – pe – re,
Pour c'est rai – sons et droi – tu – re
Que li biens d'u – ne seule heu – re
Sont de la meil – lour che – an – ce,
Ne pour – roit en nu – le guis – se

VIII

Et a chas - cun tolt et don – ne.
C'est cil qui mains s'en es – mai – e.
Que chas – cuns s'en lot et plain – gne.
Les maus d'un an a – sou – a – ge.
Qui bien sa – vroit son preu fai – re,
Le grain queil – lir sanz la pail – le.

refrain

IX

Et folle et sage est A – mours,

X

Vi – e, mors, joie et dou – lours.

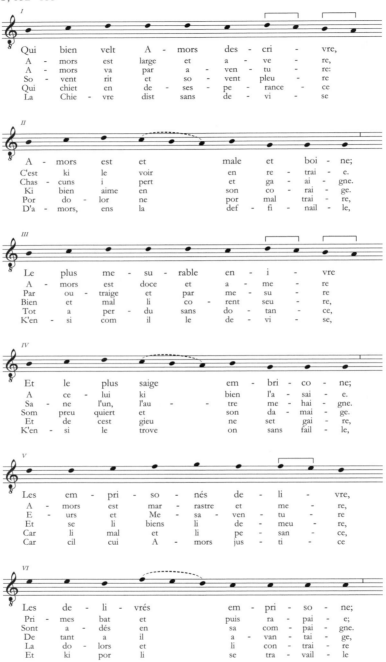

I

Qui bien velt A - mors des - cri - vre,
A - mors est large et a - ve - re,
A - mors va par a - ven - tu - re:
So - vent rit et so - vent pleu - re
Qui chiet en de - ses - pe - rance - ce
La Chie - vre dist sans de - vi - se

II

A - mors est et male et boi - ne;
C'est ki le voir en re - trai - e.
Chas - cuns i pert et ga - ai - gne.
Ki bien aime en son co - rai - ge.
Por do - lor ne por mal trai - re,
D'a - mors, ens la def - fi - nail - le,

III

Le plus me - su - rable en i - vre
A - mors est doce et a - me - re
Par ou - traige et par me - su - re
Bien et mal li co - rent seu - re,
K'en - si com il le de - vi - se,

IV

Et le plus saige em - bri - co - ne;
A ce - lui ki bien l'a - sai - e.
Sa - ne l'un, l'au - tre me - hai - gne.
Som preu quiert et son da - mai - ge.
Et de cest gieu ne set gai - re,
K'en - si le trove on sans fail - le,

V

Les em - pri - so - nés de - li - vre,
A - mors est mar - rastre et me - re,
E - urs et Me - sa - ven - tu - re
Et se li biens li de - meu - re,
Car li mal et li pe - san - ce,
Car cil cui A - mors jus - ti - ce

VI

Les de - li - vrés em - pri - so - ne;
Pri - mes bat et puis ra - pai - e;
Sont a - dés en sa com - pai - gne.
De tant a il a - van - tai - ge.
La do - lors et li con - trai - re
Et ki por li se tra - vail - le

(68) ROBERT DE REIMS

VII

L'un fait mo - rir, l'au - tre vi - vre.
Et cil ki plus le com - pe - re,
Por c'est rai - sons et droi - tu - re
Ke li bien d'u - ne seule eu - re
Sont de la mil - lor cha - an - ce,
N'em por - roit en nu - le gui - se

VIII

A l'un taut, a l'au - tre do - ne.
C'est cil ki plus s'en es - mai - e.
Ke chas - cuns s'en lot et plai - gne.
Les maus d'un an ra - so - hai - ge.
Ki bien sa - roit som preu fai - re.
Le grain coil - lir sans la pail - le.

refrain

IX

Et fole et saige est A - mors,

X

Vie et mors, joie et do - lors.

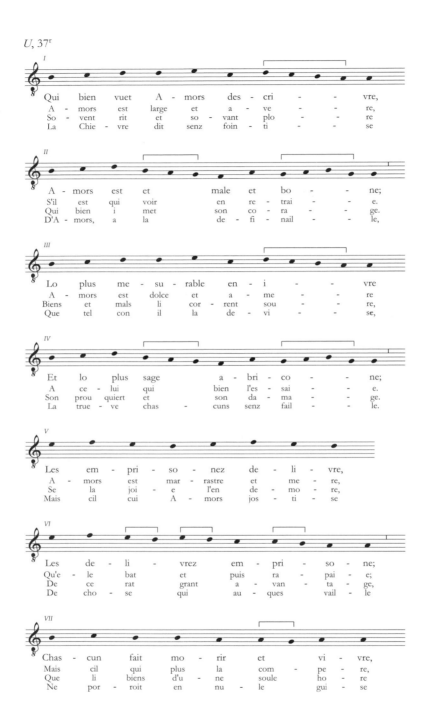

I

Qui bien vuet A - mors des - cri - - vre,
A - mors est large et a - ve - - re,
So - vent rit et so - vant plo - - re
La Chie - vre dit senz foin - ti - - se

II

A - mors est et male et bo - - ne;
S'il est qui voir en re - trai - - e.
Qui bien i met son co - ra - - ge.
D'A - mors, a la de - fi - nail - - le,

III

Lo plus me - su - rable en - i - - vre
A - mors est dolce et a - me - - re
Biens et mals li cor - rent sou - - re,
Que tel con il la de - vi - - se,

IV

Et lo plus sage a - bri - co - - ne;
A ce - lui qui bien l'es - sai - - e.
Son prou quiert et son da - ma - - ge.
La true - ve chas - cuns senz fail - - le.

V

Les em - pri - so - nez de - li - vre,
A - mors est mar - rastre et me - - re,
Se la joi - e l'en de - mo - - re,
Mais cil cui A - mors jos - ti - se

VI

Les de - li - vrez em - pri - so - ne;
Qu'e - le bat et puis ra - pai - e;
De ce - rat grant a - van - ta - ge,
De cho - se qui au - ques vail - le

VII

Chas - cun fait mo - rir et vi - vre,
Mais cil qui plus la com - pe - - re,
Que li biens d'u - ne soule ho - - re
Ne por - roit en nu - le gui - se

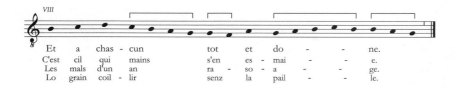

Et a chas - cun tot et do - - ne.
C'est cil qui mains s'en es - mai - - e.
Les mals d'un an ra - so - a - - ge.
Lo grain coil - lir senz la pail - - le.

CATALOGUING

Raynaud-Spanke 1655; Linker 231-9; Mölk-Wolfzettel 752,18 [837]; van den Boogaard 710

MANUSCRIPTS

X 134ᵛ–135ʳ ♫ (*Robert de rains*), *C* 113ʳ (*li chievre de rains*), *F* 115ʳ–116ʳ (empty staves), *H* 223ᵛ, *K* 189–190 ♫ (*Robert de Rains*), *M* 175ᵛ ♫ (*li chievre de rains*), *N* 90ᵛ–91ʳ ♫ (*Robert de rains*), *O* 115ᵛ–116ʳ , *P* 72ʳ⁻ᵛ ♫ (*Robert de rains*), *R* 28ʳ⁻ᵛ ♫ (*monnios*), *T* 152ᵛ–153ʳ ♫ (*kievre de rains*), *U* 37ʳ ♫ , *a* 102ᵛ ♫

PREVIOUS EDITIONS

Fauchet 1581, 140; Juvigny 1772–73, 5:424; Le Roux de Lincy 1841–42, 1:XLVIII; Tarbé 1850, 107; Dinaux 1863, 163; Brakelmann 1868b, 354; Mann 1898, 30; Mann 1899, 108; Lachèvre and Guégan 1914, 5ᵛ; Lachèvre et al. 1917, 29, 51 ♫ (French translation); Bertoni 1917, 376; Jeanroy and Långfors 1921, 29; Gennrich 1925, 436; Beck 1927, 2:267 ♫ ; Gérold 1932, 127; Gérold 1936, 293; Beck 1937, 85 ♫ ; Cremonesi 1955, 230 (Italian translation); Mary 1967, 2:6 (French translation); Tischler 1997, 11: no. 956 ♫ ; Tyssens 2015, 1:155

VERSIFICATION AND MUSICO-POETIC FORM

5, *coblas singulars* in *pedes cum cauda*; *rime dérivée* (3), *rime léonine* (1, 3), *rime paronyme* (2), *rime riche* (1–3, 5)

1	2	3	4	5	6	7	8	9	10
7a′	7b′	7a′	7b′	7a′	7b′	7a′	7b′	7C	7C

	1	2	3	4	5
a′	ivre	ere	ure	eure	ise
b′	one	aie	aigne	age	aille
c	o(u)rs				

REFRAINS

1–5.9–10 vdB 710 (without concordance)

REJECTED TEXTUAL READINGS (*X*)

1.1 descrire *(reading from CHKMNOTU)* — 2.4–5 *missing (reading from CFHKM-NOPRTUa)* — 3.1 Damors *(reading from FHKMNOPRTa)* — 4.5 demore — 4.7 hore — 5.2 en] est *(reading from FMR)*

REJECTED TEXTUAL READINGS (*R, see also Textual Variants*)

1.7 mourir] nourir — 3.1 va par] na pas — 3.7 c'est] ces — 4.4 domnage — 4.8 de un *(+1)* — 5.4 gueres — 5.7 cheanche — 6.3 De] que — 6.4 Que ainssi *(+1)*

REJECTED TEXTUAL READINGS (*T, see also Textual Variants*)

1.3 Le] la — 2.2 C'est] sest — 3.6 sa] se — 6.2 deffinaile — 6.9 la] le

TEXTUAL VARIANTS

1.1 amor *H*; descriuere *FPR*; descriuere *a* — 1.3 Le] la *T*; Les amesures e. *H*; honnorable e. *R* — 1.4 Les plus sages *H*; abricone *CU* — 1.7 Cascus *H*; Amors *O*; fait] est *F*; Lun fait m. lautre v. *MT*; morir] nourir *R* — 1.8 Alun tolt alautre done *HMT*; Amors tolt et amors d. *O* — 1.9–10 *missing in CHU* — 1.10 et mors *MOTa*; et *missing F* — 2.1–10 *appear as stanza 3 in HO, as 4 in F* — 2.1 est larage *a*; et *capital initial in a* — 2.2 C'est] sest *NT*, est *a*; Sil (Cil *H*) est ki uoir *CHMU*; Por que *O*; uos en *H*; Por uec con vou en retrai *F*; en remise *a* — 2.4 lassaie *FMTa*; b. la paie *O* — 2.6 Kelle *COU*, Car ele *FH*; puis] *missing FH*, si *O* — 2.7 Et] maix *CU,* car *F*; Cils *H*; qui] ke *C*; le] la *CFOU* — 2.8 mains] pluz *MT*; mains *copied above expunctuated* plus *N* — 2.9–10 *copied in full in a*; Et fole et sage *copied in F at end of stanzas 2–5, in T at end of 2–3, in a at end of 3–5*; Et fole *copied in MO at end of stanzas 2–5, in T at end of 4–5*; sage *followed by* et cetera *at end of stanza 5 in F*; Et fole et *copied in T at end of stanza 6* — 3.1–10 *missing in CU, appear as stanza 2 in FHO* — 3.1 *expunctuated* est *before* va *M*; va] uare *H*, na *R*; par] pas *R* — 3.2 Chascun *NPR*; Car on *F*; Luns i pert lautre i gaaigne *O*; gaiaaigne *N* — 3.4 S. lun lautre m. *MT*; En sauue len et m. *O*; chascuns *KN* — 3.6 E sunt *H*; touz jors] adies *FHMORTa*; sa] se *T* — 3.7 Preuz *followed by illegible letter* r. *H*; c'est] ce est *P*, ces *R*; raison *Pa* — 3.8 cascun *a*; et *missing H* — 3.9 Bone e male *H* — 3.10 Iois e gauz pene d. *H* — 4.1–10 *appear as stanza 3 in F* — 4.2 Ke *C*; aime en] i met *COU*, met *H* — 4.3 Biens et maus *FOU* — 4.4 et] ou *C* — 4.5 Mais *FH*; Se la ioie *CU*; Et se ioie *O*; se li] se le *H*; len d. *CFOU* — 4.6 De ceu rait grant a. *CU*; Molt en a grant a. *F*; De cel a bon a. *H*; Nen doit hair son corage *O* — 4.7 Car *F*; li] les *H*, le *N*; bien *CHNT* — 4.8 Le mal *K*; d'un] de un *R*; rasuaige *CFMTUa* — 5.1–10 *missing in Pa* — 5.1 Ie uos di tot s. *H*; s. deuise *MT* — 5.2 Damor *H*; en] a *CHOU*, est *KN*, ens *T* — 5.3 Ke teil com *COU*; Tele quil a d. *F*; Tel com cis uers le d. *H*; Quensi con *MT*; Que ce *R*; il en] il *C*, il la *MOU*, il le *T* — 5.4 Qu'ensi] einsi *MN*, que ainssi *R*; La t. chascuns s. *COU*;

Le puet lon trouer s. *F*; Tel le troueres s. *H*; trueuon *K* — 5.5 Maix *CFU*, Et *HO*; qui]
cui *MOTU* — 5.6 De chose ke (ki *FU*) aikes uaille *CFHU* — 5.7 Nen *CHMT* — 5.8
Coillir le g. *O*; g. traire *H*; la] le *T*

Manuscripts *PRTa* record an additional stanza after the fourth (presented here based
on *P*):

Qui chiet en desesperance
Por dolor et por mal trere,
Tot a perdu sanz faillance,
Ne de cel gieu ne set guere,
Car li mal et la pesance,   5.5
Les dolors et le contrere
Sont de la meillor cheance,
Qui bien savroit son gieu fere.

Anyone who falls into despair
because of pain and burdensome ills
has undoubtedly lost everything,
nor does he know much about that game [of love];
for suffering and worry,   5.5
pain and adversity
are the best things that can happen
to anyone who knows how to play his game.

Celui qui sombre dans le désespoir
de douleur et sous le poids de lourds fardeaux
a tout perdu, sans exception,
et à ce jeu [d'Amour] ne s'y entend guère,
car les maux et les soucis,   5.5
les douleurs et l'adversité
portent chance
à qui saurait jouer le jeu.

Versification

	1	2	3	4	5	6	7	8
	7a′	7b′	7a′	7b′	7a′	7b′	7a′	7b′
a′	ance							
b′	ere							

> 5.2 et] ne *RTa*; traire *RTa* — 5.3 s. dotance *T* — 5.4 Et de cest g. *T*; gueres *R*, gaire *Ta* — 5.5 li] le *R*; la] li *T* — 5.6 Les] la *Ta*; le] li *Ta*; contraire *RTa* — 5.8 son preu faire *RT*

NOTES TO THE MUSICAL TRANSCRIPTION (*X, with KNP*)

II extra b after c′ on "male" due to voicing of "-le": emended as in *NP* — III after "Le plus", d′ on "me-", d′ on "-su-", d′-c′ on "-ra-", b on "-ble", b on "en-", b-a on "-y-", b on "-vre": emended as in I — IV on "sage" last pitch untied as simple note on "-ge": emended as in II and *N*; on "enbri-", c′ and b inverted: emended as in I and *KNP* — VI *tractus* added after last pitch as in *P* — X *tractus* after "vie"; *tractus* added after last pitch as in *KP* — VII final d′ omitted: added as in V and based on the evidence of the form *pedes et versus*

NOTES TO THE MUSICAL TRANSCRIPTION (*R*)

VI, VIII *tractus* added after last pitch — VII on "-rir", extra e after g-f

NOTES TO THE MUSICAL TRANSCRIPTION (*T, with MOa [O notated a second lower]*)

I, III first five pitches are g b c′ d′ d′: emended as in *MO* — II *tractus* added after last pitch as in *MOa* — V c′ on "les": emended as in *MOa*; f′ on "-nés": emended as in *M*; f′-e′ on "de-", d′ on "-li-", e′ on "-vre": emended as in *M* — V, VII *tractus* after last pitch — VI *tractus* added after last pitch as in *MO* — VIII–X passage notated a third higher, except last pitches on "et dolors": emended after *MOa*

NOTES TO THE MUSICAL TRANSCRIPTION (*U*)

II, IV, VI, VIII *tractus* added after last pitch

MUSICAL VARIANTS (*KNP for X*)

II extra b after c′ on "male" due to voicing of "-le" *K*; b ("bo-") a-g ("-ne") *P* — III extra d′ after d′ on "-rable" due to voicing of "-ble" *KNP* — IV d′ d′/c′ ("plus") *N*; b,a,g ("sage") *KP*; b ("-ne") *N*

MUSICAL VARIANTS (*Ma for T*)

I, III first five pitches are g b c′ d′ d′ *a* — I d′/c′ ("-cri") *M* — II b-c′ ("male"), b-a ("et") *M* — III extra d′ after c′ ("en-") due to voicing of previous "-ble" *a*; d′ d′/c′ ("-i-") *M* — IV extra a after g ("em-") due to voicing of previous "-ge" *a*; b-a ("-bri-") *M* — V f′ ("-nés") f′-e′ ("de-") d′ ("-li-") e′ ("-vre") *a* — VI phrase is e′ ("les") f′ ("de-") e′ ("-li-") d′ ("-vrés") e′ ("-em-") d′,c′,b ("-pri-") a ("-so-") a ("-ne") *M* — VII phrase is d′ ("cas-") d′ ("-cun") d′ ("fait") e′ ("mo-") f′ ("-rir") g′ ("et") f′-e′ ("vi-") d′ ("-vre") a; d′ ("-rir") e′-f′ ("l'au-") g′ g′/f′ ("-tre") e′ ("vi-") M — VIII phrase is d′ ("et") d′ ("a") e′ ("cas-") d′ ("-cun") c′ ("taut") b-a ("et") g ("dou-") g ("-ne") a — IX b ("et") a ("saige") b ("est") b,a,g ("A-") M — X d′ d′/c′ ("mors") b,a,g ("joie") a ("et") b-g ("do-") M

COMMENTARY

The melody of this song varies according to the quite different readings in the sources. These show four main branches: *KNPX*, *R*, *MOTa*, and *U*, leading us to present four separate editions of the music. In every instance but one, the listed corrections and musical variants are restricted to that one branch. The exception concerns the variants in *O*, which are too numerous (and may be viewed in Tischler 1997). *R* offers, as usual, a wholly idiosyncratic version. The other three families show a common melody for the *pedes* but then diverge considerably in the *cauda*. Note that the version in *U*, very close to Robert de Reims's period of activity, fails to include refrain vdB 710, just like *CH*; and the abundant ornamentation in the final phrase of *U* shows it to be the song's concluding statement. We may thus see the refrain as a later addition to the work, a fact further indicated by its lack of influence on the rest of the song (see Introduction). Finally, the divergence of the refrain melodies across the families suggests that the refrain constitutes a solely textual quotation, or else is simply not a quotation. — The attribution to Moniot d'Arras in manuscript *R* has been rejected (Petersen Dyggve 1938, 24). Manuscript *O* bears a marginal comment added in a later hand at the incipit: "3. Chanson de Robert de Reims selon Fauchet." Similarly, in the right margin of *R*, at the incipit, an early modern hand attributes this song to "Robert de Rheims," with bibliographical reference to Fauchet. — 5.1–10 There appears to be a leaf missing in manuscript *a*, where fol. cxvi (in the contemporaneous foliation) is immediately followed by fol. cxviii; this may account for the missing last stanza. — There is clear textual overlap between three of this song's stanzas and the lyric insertion (representing the voice of the Bride) found after line 1272 in the anonymous *Cantiques Salemon*. For a detailed analysis of the borrowings (shared paradoxes and rhyme words, especially), see Hunt 2006, 58–61.

4a   Quant voi le douz tens venir   Chanson avec des refrains

Quant voi le douz tens venir,
La flor en la pree,
La rose espanir,
Adonc chant, plor et sospir,
Tant ai joie amee,   1.5
Dont ne puis joïr.
Mir
Ma joie sans repentir,
Tir
A ce que ne puis sentir;   1.10
N'assentir
Ne me puis, por nul avoir,
Au departir.
Je voi ce que je desir,
Si n'en puis joie avoir.   1.15

Quant plus regart et remir
Sa color rosee,
De duel cuit morir,
Car ja n'i cuit avenir,
Las! et tant m'agree   2.5
Que n'en puis partir.
Ha!
Deus! porrai je tant servir
Que
Nue la puisse tenir   2.10
A loisir?
Je non ce croi,
Car ne li ert a plaisir.
Que que m'en doie avenir,
Je l'aim sans decevoir.   2.15

Se j'aim flor et rose et lis
Et sage et senee,
Ce m'est joie et pris!
Molt en aim mon cuer et pris
Quant ot en pensee   3.5

De ce qu'a enpris.
Pris
M'ont si oil et si doz ris;
Mis
M'a en chartre et entrepris   3.10
Ses clers vis;
Sa grant biauté et s'amor
M'a si espris
Que mort sui sanz avoir pis,
Se de li n'ai secors.   3.15

4a   ❧

When I see the fair season arrive,
flowers in the meadow,
roses in bloom,
that's when I sing, weep, and sigh,
so eager for joy have I been—   1.5
joy I cannot have.
I look back
on my joy with no regret,
I am drawn
to that which I cannot experience;   1.10
not for any gain
can I accept
this farewell.
I see what I desire,
yet cannot experience joy.   1.15

The more I observe and admire
her rosy complexion,
[the more] I think I'll die of grief,
for I do not expect ever to approach her,
alas! but she is so attractive to me   2.5
that I cannot leave her.
Ah!

God! Will my devotion ever
enable
me to hold her naked,   2.10
as I wish?
I don't think so,
for she'll never agree to it.
Whatever may happen to me,
I love her sincerely.   2.15

If I love flowers and roses and lilies,
and a wise and sensible [woman],
I have my joy and reward!
I love and value my heart
for having thought of   3.5
what it has undertaken.
Captured
have I been by her eyes and gentle laugh;
seized
have I been and imprisoned   3.10
by her radiant face;
her great beauty and [my] love for her
have so captivated me
that I am dead if not worse,
unless she comes to my rescue.   3.15

4a   ∂ۇ

Quand je vois venir la belle saison,
la fleur dans la prairie,
la rose s'épanouir,
alors je chante, pleure et soupire,
tant j'ai connu une joie   1.5
dont je ne puis plus jouir.
Je réfléchis
à cette joie sans regret;
je suis attiré

par ce que je ne puis sentir;   1.10
et je ne puis accepter,
à nul prix,
cette séparation.
Je vois ce que je désire,
sans pouvoir en jouir.   1.15

Plus je regarde et admire
son teint rosé,
plus je crois mourir de chagrin,
car je ne pourrai jamais m'approcher d'elle,
hélas! et elle me plaît tant   2.5
que je ne puis la quitter.
Ah!
Dieu! pourrai-je la servir
au point de
pouvoir la tenir nue   2.10
à mon aise?
Je ne le crois pas,
car elle n'y consentira jamais.
Quoi qu'il doive m'en arriver,
je l'aime de tout cœur.   2.15

Si j'aime la fleur et la rose et le lys,
et la sage et la sensée,
c'est pour moi une joie et un prix!
J'aime tant mon cœur et le prise
pour avoir pensé   3.5
à ce qu'il a entrepris.
Ses yeux et son doux sourire m'ont
captivé;
son visage radieux m'a
saisi   3.10
et mis en prison;
sa grande beauté et l'amour qu'elle inspire
se sont tant emparés de moi
que je mourrai (et même pire)
si elle ne vient à mon secours.   3.15

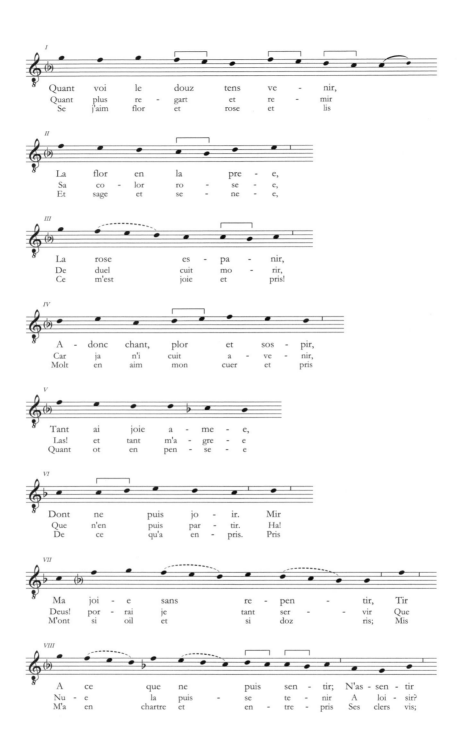

I

Quant voi le douz tens ve - nir,
Quant plus re - gart et re - mir
Se j'aim flor et rose et lis

II

La flor en la pre - e,
Sa co - lor ro - se - e,
Et sage et se - ne - e,

III

La rose es - pa - nir,
De duel cuit mo - rir,
Ce m'est joie et pris!

IV

A - donc chant, plor et sos - pir,
Car ja n'i cuit a - ve - nir,
Molt en aim mon cuer et pris

V

Tant ai joie a - me - e,
Las! et tant m'a - gre - e
Quant ot en pen - se - e

VI

Dont ne puis jo - ir. Mir
Que n'en puis par - tir. Ha!
De ce qu'a en - pris. Pris

VII

Ma joi - e sans re - pen - tir, Tir
Deus! por - rai je tant ser - vir Que
M'ont si oil et si doz ris; Mis

VIII

A ce que ne puis sen - tir; N'as - sen - tir
Nu - e la puis - se te - nir A loi - sir?
M'a en chartre et en - tre - pris Ses clers vis;

IX

Ne me puis, por nul a - voir,
Je non ce croi, Car ne li
Sa grant biau - té et s'a - mor

X

Au de - par - tir.
ert a plai - sir.
M'a si es - pris

XI

Je voi ce que je de - sir,
Que que m'en doie a - ve - nir,
Que mort sui sanz a - voir pis,

XII

Si n'en puis joie a - voir.
Je l'aim sans de - ce - voir.
Se de li n'ai se - cors.

CATALOGUING

Raynaud-Spanke 1485; Linker 231-8; Mölk-Wolfzettel 576,1 [575]; van den Boogaard 1149/1580

MANUSCRIPTS

X 135^{r-v} ♪ (*Robert de rains*), *K* 190–191 ♪ (*Robert de rains*), *N* 91^{r} ♪ (*Robert de rains*), *P* 72^{v}–73^{r} ♪ (*Robert de rains*)

MATERIAL

Stanza 1, XI–XII (lines 14–15): vdB 1149. Same music in part 235 of motet Ludwig *Qant voi le douz* (235) / LATUS (M14): see motet version (4b). Same music for line 1 in song RS 73, st. 5 *Ier main pensis chevauchai*: *M* 99^{v}, *T* 44^{v}; att. Ernoul Caupain (*T*) or Baude de la Quarriere (*M*) or Jehan Erart (*M* [table])
Stanza 2, XI–XII (lines 14–15): vdB 1580. With music in part 822 of motet Ludwig *Face de moi son pleisir* (822) / DOMINO or OMNES (M13): *Mo* 235^{v}, *W*$_{2}$ 231^{r}

PREVIOUS EDITIONS

Tarbé 1850, 102; Mann 1898, 25; Mann 1899, 103; Lachèvre and Guégan 1914, 7^{r}; Lachèvre et al. 1917, 30, 52 ♪ (French translation); Gennrich 1926–27, 29 ♪; Tischler 1997, 10: no. 847 ♪

3, *coblas doblas* in *oda continua*; *rime dérivée* (1, 3), *rime en écho* (1, 3), *rime homonyme* (3), *rime identique* (1–2), *rime léonine* (1–3), *rime paronyme* (1), *rime riche* (1–3)

	1	2	3	4	5	6	7	8	9	10	11	12	13	14	15
1	7a	5b′	5a	7a	5b′	5a	1a	7a	1a	7a	3a	7c	4a	*7a*	6c
2	7a	5b′	5a	7a	5b′	5a	1x	7a	1y	7a	3a	4c	7a	*7a*	6c
3	7a	5b′	5a	7a	5b′	5a	1a	7a	1a	7a	3a	7c	4a	7a	6c

	1	2	3
a	ir	ir	is
b′	ee	ee	ee
c	oir	oi(r)	or(s)
x		a	
y		mute [e]	

REFRAINS

1.14–15 vdB 1149 *(see concordances in Material)* — 2.14–15 vdB 1580 *(see concordances in Material)*

REJECTED TEXTUAL READINGS

See motet version (4b)

1.6 Dont ie ne (+1) *(reading from KNPClMo[1]Mo[2]W₂)* — 2.1 rega *remainder of word barely legible* — 2.7 Ha *added* (−1) — 2.8 Deus] dex — 2.12 ce] se *(reading from KNP)* — 3.5–6 *missing (reading after KNP)*

TEXTUAL VARIANTS

See motet version (4b)

1.3 rosee *Cl* — 1.4 chant] pens *ClMo[2]* — 1.5 Tant] qant *Mo[1]W₂*; joie] cele *W₂* — 1.6 Si nen puis *Mo[1]* — 1.9 Tir *missing Mo[2]* — 1.10 ne] me *Mo[2]* — 1.11 Assentir *ClMo[1]Mo[2]W₂* — 1.12 me] mi *P*, men *W₂*; por] par *Cl*; nul avoir] nul auenir *Cl*, nule rien (riens *W₂*) *Mo[1]W₂* — 1.13 Au (a *Mo[2]*) repentir *ClMo[1]Mo[2]* — 1.14 Car ie *Cl* — 1.15 avoir] auenir *Cl* — 2.7 Ha *missing KNP* — 2.13 Que ne *K*; ert] est *N* — 3.6 ce *missing KN* — 3.12 biauté *missing N* — 3.13 sorpris *P* — 3.14 mort] mors *K*; pis] pris *P*

NOTES TO THE MUSICAL TRANSCRIPTION

III f′ on "La": emended as in *ClFMo[1]W₂* (*see motet version*); *tractus* added after last pitch as in *KNP* — V extra b after last pitch: emended as in *ClFMo[1]W₂* — VI c′ on "dont", c′-d′ on "je", d′ on "ne": emended as in *KNP*; *tractus* on both sides of last pitch added — VII ligature bridging d´ and c´ on "-pen-" added as in *KNP*; *tractus* on both sides of last pitch added as in *KNP* — VIII *tractus* added after last pitch as in *KN* — XII extra a appears after a on "joie" due to voicing of "-e": emended as in *KNP*; triple *tractus* signaling end of stanza after last pitch and syllable

MUSICAL VARIANTS
See also motet version (4b)
I–V (up to "a-") no B♭ signature *KNP* — III f´ ("La") *KNP* — V extra b after last pitch *KNP*

COMMENTARY
The motet (4b) clearly predates the song (4a), which is a later adaptation and continuation of it by an anonymous hand (see Introduction). Various metrical and musical discrepancies bolster the argument that stanzas 2 and 3 are exogenous additions. In particular, stanza 2 is irregular in several respects. First, Robert's intensive use of echo rhyming is part of his stylistic signature, and yet lines 2.7 and 2.9 do not exhibit the echo rhymes found in the corresponding lines of stanzas 1 and 3. In fact, line 2.7 is missing altogether in all four manuscript witnesses (the interjection *Ha!* is an editorial conjecture). Line 2.9 shows nothing more than the so-called "mute [e]"; the latter is to be treated like the final syllable of a feminine rhyme, which is ordinarily identified by a mere apostrophe. Furthermore, line 2.12 is three syllables short, while line 2.13 is three syllables long, consequently creating an overlap in the music/text structure of the passage. Contrary to previous editors (notably Tarbé 1850 and Mann 1898/1899), who offer fanciful reconstructions of lines 2.12–13, we retain the apparently faulty readings because the combined syllable count of these two lines is the same as in stanzas 1 and 3. — 2.14–15, XI–XII The music of refrain vdB 1580 in stanza 2 is not copied in the song sources, but the text of the refrain fits the music of refrain vdB 1149 of stanza 1. Refrain vdB 1580 also appears in motet Ludwig 822 with different music; however, this music is not suitable for our song because the second line of the refrain in the motet has four syllables ("je l'amerai"), whereas the line is hexasyllabic in our song. — 3.14, XI See Commentary on song no. 1, line 1.5, V.

4b   Qant voi le douz tens venir / (IMMO)LATUS   Motet

Motetus
Qant voi le douz tens venir,
la flor en la pree,
la rose espanir,
adonc chant, plor et soupir,
qant ai cele amee   5
dont ne puis joïr.
Mir
ma joie sanz repentir,
tir
a ce qe ne puis sentir;   10
assentir
ne m'en puis, por nule riens,
au departir.
Je voi ce qe je desir,
si n'en puis joie avoir.   15

Tenor
(IMMO)LATUS

4b   ঞ

When I see the fair season arrive,
flowers in the meadow,
roses in bloom,
that's when I sing, weep, and sigh,
for I'm in love with the one   5
I cannot have.
I look back
on my joy without regret,
I am drawn
to that which I cannot experience;   10
not for anything
can I accept

this farewell.
I see what I desire,
yet cannot experience joy.   15

4b   ✥

Quand je vois venir la belle saison,
la fleur dans la prairie,
la rose s'épanouir,
alors je chante, pleure et soupire,
car j'ai aimé celle   5
dont je ne puis plus jouir.
Je réfléchis
à cette joie sans regret;
je suis attiré
par ce que je ne puis sentir;   10
je ne puis accepter,
à nul prix,
cette séparation.
Je vois ce que je désire,
sans pouvoir en jouir.   15

CATALOGUING

Ludwig *Qant voi le douz* (235) / LATUS (M14); Linker 265-637

MANUSCRIPTS

W₂ 245^(r–v) ♪; with triplum *En mai quant rose* (236): *Mo* 203^v–204^r ♪ (*Mo[2]*) (empty staves in the motetus); with triplum as motetus and motetus as triplum: *Cl* 382^v ♪, *Mo* 167^v–168^r ♪ (*Mo[1]*); as clausula LATUS: *F* 158^v ♪ (music only)

MATERIAL

Motetus. Perf. 39–46 (lines 14–15): vdB 1149. Same music in song RS 1485, st. 1 *Quant voi le dous tens venir (La flor)*: see song version (4a). Same music for line 1 in song RS 73, st. 5 *Ier main pensis chevauchai*: see Material in 4a
Tenor. Melisma from *Alleluia ℣ Pascha nostrum*, Easter Sunday; biblical reference: Cor. 5:7

PREVIOUS EDITIONS

Jacobsthal 1880, 48; Raynaud 1881–83, 1:104; Gennrich 1926–27, 29 ♪; Rokseth 1935–39, 2: no. 121 ♪; Anderson and Close 1975, no. 32 ♪; Tischler 1978–85, 2: no. 121 ♪; Tischler 1982, 2: no. 224 ♪; Thomas 1985–89, 2: no. 8 ♪ (English translation)

VERSIFICATION

	1	2	3	4	5	6	7	8	9	10	11	12	13	14	15
	7a	5b′	5a	7a	5b′	5a	1a	7a	1a	7a	3a	7x	4a	*7a*	*6y*
a	ir														
b′	ee														
x	iens														
y	oir														

REFRAINS

14–15 vdB 1149 *(see concordances in Material)*

REJECTED TEXTUAL READINGS

Tenor. Latus *missing Mo[2]*

TEXTUAL VARIANTS

Motetus. See song version (4a)
Tenor. Latus est *F*

Rhythmic mode after *ClFMo[1]Mo[2]*

Motetus (*Mo[2]* missing). Perf. 16 e′ on "cele": emended as in *ClFMo[1]* — Perf. 23 d′ on "sanz"; emended as in *ClFMo[1]* — Perf. 34 c′/d′ on "puis", d′ on "por": emended as in *ClMo[1]* — Perf. 40–41 d′-e′ on "qe", f′ on "je", e,d′,c′ on "de-"; emended after *ClFMo[1]* — Perf. 43 pitches notated a second higher: emended as in *ClMo[1]* — Perf. 44–45 a-g-a on "joie", b on "a-": emended after *Mo[1]*

MUSICAL VARIANTS

See also song version (4a)

Motetus. Perf. 1 to end no B♭ signature *ClMo[1]* — Perf. 1 g′-f′ ("voi") *ClMo[1]* — Perf. 4 c′ ("-nir") then *tractus Cl* — Perf. 6 d′-c′ ("en") *ClF* — Perf. 9 c′ b *F* — Perf. 17 c′-b ("-e") *ClMo[1]* — Perf. 18 c′ d′ *F* — Perf. 19 e′ ("jo-") *ClF*; f′,e′,d′ ("jo-") *Mo[1]* — Perf. 24 e′/f′ ("re-") *ClMo[1]* — Perf. 28 e′/f′ ("qe") *ClMo[1]* — Perf. 29 e′ ("sen-") *ClMo[1]*; d′ b *F* — Perf. 31 a c′ b *F* — Perf. 33 b ("ne") *ClMo[1]* — Perf. 34 b d′ *F* — Perf. 35 c′ a *F* — Perf. 39 c′-b ("voi") *ClMo[1]* — Perf. 40 c′ d *F* — Perf. 43 b unplicated *F*; b-a *Cl* — Perf. 44 g ("joie") *ClMo[1]* — Perf. 45–46 a ("a-"), b ("-ve-"), c′ ("-nir") *Cl*

Tenor. Perf. 1–22 passage missing *Mo[2]* — Perf. 9–24 no B♭ signature *Cl* — Perf. 27 to end: no B♭ signature *Mo[1]* — Perf. 33–34 *ordo* omitted *F* — Perf. 35–36 these pitches separated by *tractus Cl* — Perf. 43 *tractus* after this pitch *ClMo[1]Mo[2]*

5a   L'autrier de jouste un rivage   Pastourelle

L'autrier de jouste un rivage,
Trespensis a fine amor,
Erroie par un herbage
Por conforter ma dolor.
Si vi seule en un destor   1.5
Pastorele cointe et sage
De molt bel ator;
Chief ot blont, les euz rians
Et fresche la color.
Au plus tost que j'onques pos,   1.10
Vers li ma voie tor.
En sa main tint un tabor,
Et tant me plot que sans sejor,
De si loing con je la vi,
Li presentai m'amor.   1.15

Je la salu doucement,
Lez li tout maintenant m'assis,
Et ele leus le me rent.
Puis, aprés mon voloir, li dis:
"Bele, je sui vostre amis;   2.5
Se de moi avez talent,
Touz iere a vo devis."
"Sire, mercis vos en rent.
Més trop feroie pis,
Se Robin, que j'aime tant,   2.10
Laissoie, ce m'est vis;
De m'amor est trop sorpris,
Et je de la soe ensement.
Onques més ne les senti,
Les maus d'amer, més or les sent."   2.15

"Bele, tout ce n'a mestier,
Més faites ce que je vos di!
Donés moi sans racointier
Vostre amor par vostre merci,
Si laissiez vostre berchier!"   3.5

"Certes, sire, trop l'ai chier.
Tout a un mot vos di,
Ne·l vueill por autrui changier.
A moi avés failli!
Més alés vos en arrier,   3.10
Qu'il ne vos truist ici!
Je l'atent souz ce pomier
Delez le bos vert et flori.
Ainz li bois ne m'ennuia,
Ne moi ne mon ami."   3.15

5a   ❧

The other day, by a riverbank,
intent upon true love,
I was wandering through a meadow
to find comfort for my pain.
In a secluded spot, I saw, all by herself,   1.5
a cheerful and sensible shepherdess
who looked very attractive;
she had blond hair, smiling eyes,
and a fresh complexion.
As soon as I could,   1.10
I started off in her direction.
In her hand, she held a tabor,
and she was so appealing that, with no delay,
no sooner had I seen her,
I offered her my love.   1.15

I greeted her sweetly,
immediately sat down beside her,
and she raised no objection.
Then, with my desire in mind, I said to her:
"Dear girl, I'm yours!   2.5
If you find me appealing,
I'm at your command."

"Sir, I thank you.
But it would be very wrong of me,
I'm sure, to leave Robin,   2.10
whom I love very much;
he is quite taken with me,
as I am with him.
Never before have I felt
the pangs of love, but I feel them now."   2.15

"Dear girl, none of that matters;
just do as I say!
Grant me your love
graciously, without further ado,
and give up your shepherd!"   3.5
"No, sir, he is too dear to me.
In a word, I tell you,
I don't care to trade him for anyone else.
Your attempt to woo me has failed!
Now go back to where you were,   3.10
lest he find you here!
I expect him under that apple tree
beside the green, flowering woods.
My love and I have never
disliked this grove."   3.15

5a   ⁊

L'autre jour, le long d'un rivage,
préoccupé par fine amour,
j'errais dans une prairie
pour apaiser ma douleur.
Je vis, toute seule dans un détour,   1.5
une bergère gracieuse et sensée,
très bien habillée;
elle avait les cheveux blonds, les yeux riants
et le teint frais.

Aussi vite que possible,   1.10
je dirige mes pas vers elle.
Dans la main elle tenait un tambour,
et elle me plut tant que, sans tarder,
d'aussi loin que je la vis,
je lui déclarai mon amour.   1.15

Je la salue gentiment;
je m'assieds tout de suite à son côté,
elle me rend mon salut aussitôt.
Puis, pensant à mon désir, je lui dis:
"Belle, je suis votre ami;   2.5
si vous me trouvez à votre gré,
je m'en remettrai à votre commandement."
"Sire, je vous en remercie;
mais j'agirais bien mal,
me semble-t-il, si je quittais Robin   2.10
que j'aime tant.
Il est amoureux de moi,
tout comme je le suis de lui.
Jamais je ne les ai sentis,
les maux d'amour, mais maintenant je les sens."   2.15

"Belle, tout ça n'a aucune importance;
faites juste ce que je vous dis!
Donnez-moi votre amour
sans chicaner, je vous prie,
et laissez là votre berger!"   3.5
"Non, sire, il m'est trop cher;
en un mot, je vous le dis:
je n'ai pas l'intention de le remplacer.
Vous ne m'avez pas séduite!
Non, allez-vous-en,   3.10
qu'il ne vous trouve pas ici!
Je l'attends sous ce pommier
du côté de ce bois vert et fleuri.
Ce bois ne nous a jamais déplu,
ni à moi ni à mon ami."   3.15

Stanza 1

Stanzas 2 and 3

IV

Puis,   a - prés   mon   vo - loir,   li   dis:
Vostre   a - mor   par   vos - tre   mer - ci,

V

"Be - le,   je   sui   vostre   a - mis;
Si   lais - siez   vos - tre   ber - chier!"

VI

Se   de   moi   a - vez   ta - lent,
"Cer - tes,   si - re,   trop   l'ai   chier.

VII

Touz   iere   a   vo   de - vis."
Tout   a   un   mot   vos   di,

VIII

"Si - re,   mer - cis   vos   en   rent.
Ne·l   vueill   por   au - trui   chan - gier.

IX

Més   trop   fe - roi - e   pis,
A   moi   a - vés   fail - li!

X

Se   Ro - bin,   que   j'ai - me   tant,
Més   a - lés   vos   en   ar - rier,

XI

Lais - soi - e,   ce   m'est   vis;
Qu'il   ne   vos   truist   i - ci!

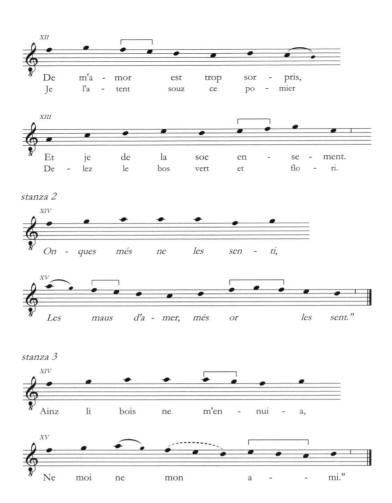

XII
De m'a - mor est trop sor - pris,
Je l'a - tent souz ce po - mier

XIII
Et je de la soe en - se - ment.
De - lez le bos vert et flo - ri.

stanza 2

XIV
On - ques més ne les sen - ti,

XV
Les maus d'a - mer, més or les sent."

stanza 3

XIV
Ainz li bois ne m'en - nui - a,

XV
Ne moi ne mon a - mi."

CATALOGUING

Raynaud-Spanke 35, 44a; Linker 231-4; Mölk-Wolfzettel 937,1 [1442]; van den Boogaard
1424

MANUSCRIPTS

X 189ᵛ–190ʳ 🎵 (*Robert de rains*)

MATERIAL

Stanza 2, XIV–XV (lines 14–15): vdB 1424. With music in part 659 of motet Ludwig
Par un matinet l'autrier (658) / *He sire que voz vantez* (659) / *E bergier si grant* (657) /

FLOS FILIUS EIUS (O16): *Cl* 389ʳ, *Mo* 27ᵛ. Without music in song RS 962, st. 7 *L'au-trier par un matinet (Erroie)*: *K* 243, *M* 100ʳ, *P* 93ʳ, *T* 46ᵛ, *X* 165ʳ; without this st. and refrain: *N* 119ʳ, att. Jehan de Neuville (*MT*) or Colart le Boutellier (*NPX*) or Jehan Erart (*M* [table]). Without music in text *D'amour et de jalousie*: line 315

PREVIOUS EDITIONS
Tarbé 1850, 105; Mann 1898, 21; Mann 1899, 99; Lachèvre and Guégan 1914, 8ʳ; Lachèvre et al. 1917, 31, 53 ♫ (French translation); Paden 1987, 220 (English translation); Tischler 1997, 1: no. 25 ♫

VERSIFICATION AND MUSICO-POETIC FORM
3, *coblas singulars* in *pedes cum cauda*; *rime annexée* (3), *rime dérivée* (1–2), *rime iden-tique* (1–3), *rime léonine* (1–2), *rime paronyme* (3), *rime riche* (1–3)

	1	2	3	4	5	6	7	8	9	10	11	12	13	14	15
1	7a′	7b	7a′	7b	7b	7a′	5b	7x	6b	7y	6b	7b	8b	7c	6b
2	7a	8b	7a	8b	7b	7a	6b	7a	6b	7a	6b	7b	8a	*7c*	*8a*
3	7a	8b	7a	8b	7a	7a	6b	7a	6b	7a	6b	7a	8b	7c	6b

	1	2	3
a(′)	age	ent	ier
b	or	is	i
c	i	i	a
x	ans		
y	os		

REFRAINS
2.14–15 vdB 1424 *(see concordances in Material)*

REJECTED TEXTUAL READINGS
2.10 iaim *(−1)* — 3.8 Ne le *(+1)* — 3.10 arriere *(+1)*

NOTES TO THE MUSICAL TRANSCRIPTION
Stanzas 1–3. III *tractus* after g′ on "-e": postponed after last pitch — V extra e′ after e′ on "seule" due to voicing of "-le" — XIII *tractus* added after last pitch — XV triple *tractus* signaling end of stanza after last pitch and syllable
Stanzas 2–3. I, III ligature bridging d′ and c′ on "-ce" added to accommodate the line *(see Commentary below)* — II ligature bridging e′ and f′ on "tout main-" removed to accommodate the line *(id.)* — IV on "voloir", ligature bridging e′ and d′ removed to accommodate the line *(id.)* — VI ligature bridging d′ and e′ on "-vez" added to

accommodate the line (*id.*) — VII ligature bridging f′ and e′ on "a vos" removed to accommodate the line (*id.*)

Stanza 2. XIV–XV music added as in *Mo (see Material above and Commentary below)* with a transposition an octave higher

Stanza 3. XIV–XV music added as in stanza 1 *(see Commentary below)*

MUSICAL VARIANTS
See motet version (5b)

COMMENTARY
The motet (5b) clearly predates the song (5a), which is a later adaptation and continuation of it by an anonymous hand. Indeed, the melodic morphology of the motetus is typical of the polyphonic settings on DOMINO QUONIAM, and stanzas 2–3 are exogenous additions that show versification, structure, and poetic quality differing from those of the first (see further Commentary below and Introduction). — In stanzas 2–3, the feminine rhymes of stanza 1 become masculine (lines 1, 3, and 6), thereby taking up the equivalent of seven notes instead of eight with the effacement of the unstressed final *-e*. In order to compensate for the shrinkage of lines 1, 3, and 6, the continuator of the text lengthened the lines that follow (2, 4, and 7) by giving each an extra syllable and, in so doing, rendered the musical phrases and poetic lines out of phase with each other. Thus, stanzas 2–3 do not exhibit scribal errors in copying; rather, they appear to have been structurally flawed since their inception. By conjecturally adding or removing some ligatures in stanzas 2 and 3 (see Notes to the Musical Transcription), our intention is to arrive at a version that is functional and suitable for performance. — 2.14–15, XIV–V The music of the refrain of stanza 2 has been borrowed from its concordance in *Mo*; note the sameness of the melodies of the last distich of stanza 1 and of the refrain of stanza 2. — 3.14–15, XIV–V Whether or not the last two lines of stanza 3 constitute a refrain is uncertain. The position of this material at the end of the stanza in a song that has at least one refrain-quotation (in stanza 2) suggests that it may be borrowed. On the other hand, these lines exhibit no divergence in versification from the corresponding (non-refrain) lines in stanza 1; furthermore, they occasion no break in syntax or shift in lyric voice, all of which are common features of refrains. Additionally, they have no known textual or musical concordances. This distich has been set to the music of the last distich of stanza 1, with which it shares the same metrical scheme. Note that if these two lines constituted a refrain, they were probably sung to their own melody.

En sa main tint un ta - bor, et tant me plot que sans se - jor,

de si loing con je la vi, li pre - sen - tai m'a - mor.

CATALOGUING

Ludwig *L'autrier de jouste un rivage* (133a) / DOMINO QUONIAM (M13)

MANUSCRIPTS

W_2 189^v–190^r ♫ with Latin text *Virgo gignit genitorem* [Ludwig 133]; as clausula DOMINO QUONIAM: *F* 156^r ♫ (music only)

MATERIAL

Tenor. Melisma from gradual *Hec dies* ℣ *Confitemini domino*, Easter Sunday; biblical reference: Ps. 117:24 ℣ Ps. 117:1

VERSIFICATION

	1	2	3	4	5	6	7	8	9	10	11	12	13	14	15
	7a′	7b	7a′	7b	7b	7a′	5b	7x	6b	7y	6b	7b	8b	7z	6b

a′	age
b	or
x	ans
y	os
z	i

REJECTED TEXTUAL READINGS

Tenor. Domino quoniam] Domino W_2

NOTES TO THE MUSICAL TRANSCRIPTION

Rhythmic mode after *F*

Motetus. Perf. 4 *tractus* added as at perf. 12

Tenor. Perf. 57 extra ordo e′ d′ follows

MUSICAL VARIANTS

See also song version (5a)

Motetus. Perf. 6 e′/f′ g′ *F* — Perf. 23 d′ e′ *F* — Perf. 26 f′/e f′ *F* — Perf. 27 g′ g′/a′ *F* — Perf. 29 d′ f′ *F* — Perf. 30 e′ c′ *F* — Perf. 31 a b *F* — Perf. 52 a′/g′ f′ *F*

Tenor. Perf. 39–41 these pitches as one ordo *F*

COMMENTARY

See also Commentary on 5a

The work presented here is the restoration of the now-lost French motet *L'autrier de jouste un rivage* (133a) / DOMINO QUONIAM (M13); this reconstruction is based on the music of the corresponding motet *Virgo gignit genitorem* (Ludwig 133) / DOMINO QUONIAM (M13) in *W₂*, and the text of the song *L'autrier de jouste un rivage* in *X*. The correspondence between the French song and the Latin motet had hitherto escaped notice, and according to the evidence offered by the analysis of the different arrangements of this work, there is no doubt that the original setting was the French motet presented here, and that the French song, the clausula, and the Latin motet are later arrangements (see Introduction).

Touse de vile champestre
Pestre
Ses aigniaus menot,
Et n'ot
Fors un sien chiennet en destre.   1.5
Estre
Vousist par semblant,
En enblant,
La ou Robins flajolot.
Et ot   1.10
La vois, qui respont
Et espont
La note d'un dorenlot.

Quant Robins vit la pucele,
Cele
Vint a lui riant.
Atant
Acole la damoisele.   2.5
Ele
Le tret dou sentier,
Car entier
Ot son cuer et son talent.
Alant   2.10
Ont fait maint trestor
Et entor
Entracolant et balant.

Dist Robins: "Se je savoie
Voie,
Qu'autres ne seüst,
S'eüst
M'amie a mengier a joie   3.5
Oie
Et gastiaus pevrez,
Abevrez
A un grant hanap de fust,

Et fust   3.10
Li vins formentieus
Et itieus
Que la bele ne·l refust!"

6   🙦

A village shepherdess
took her lambs
out to pasture,
accompanied
only by a little dog of hers at her right side.   1.5
Apparently,
she would have liked,
as she walked on,
to be where Robin was playing his flute.
He heard   1.10
her voice, as she repeatedly
sang
the tune of a refrain.

When Robin saw the young girl,
she
came toward him, smiling.
At that,
he embraced the girl.   2.5
She
drew him off the path,
since her heart and desire
were set wholly on him.
As they went along,   2.10
they made many a twist
and turn,
embracing each other and dancing.

Said Robin, "If I knew
a way
no one else knew,
my love would have
the pleasure of eating   3.5
goose
and peppered cakes,
downed
with a wooden goblet brimming with drink,
and [the drink] would be   3.10
fermented wine
so tasty
that the maiden would not refuse it!"

6   🙠

Une jeune fille d'un village de campagne
menait
paître ses agneaux,
accompagnée
seulement de son petit chien, à sa droite.   1.5
Elle semblait
vouloir se rendre,
en déambulant,
là où Robin jouait de sa petite flûte.
[Robin] entend   1.10
sa voix, qui entonne
et répète
l'air d'un refrain.

Quand Robin voit la pucelle,
elle
vient vers lui en riant.
Sur ce,
il embrasse la demoiselle.   2.5
Elle

l'attire hors du sentier,
car elle le désirait
de tout son cœur.
Chemin faisant,   2.10
ils font bien des tours
et des pirouettes
en s'embrassant, en dansant.

Robin dit: "Si je savais comment
obtenir
ce qu'aucun berger ne peut se procurer,
mon amie
aurait le plaisir de manger   3.5
de l'oie
et des gâteaux poivrés,
accompagnés
d'un grand gobelet en bois,
et il y aurait   3.10
un vin fermenté
tel
que la belle ne le refuserait pas!"

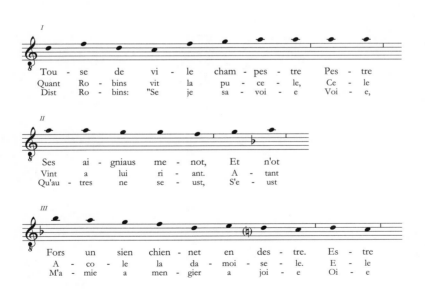

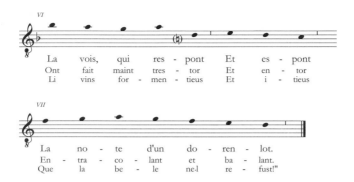

VI

La vois, qui res - pont Et es - pont
Ont fait maint tres - tor Et en - tor
Li vins for - men - tieus Et i - tieus

VII

La no - te d'un do - ren - lot.
En - tra - co - lant et ba - lant.
Que la be - le ne·l re - fust!"

CATALOGUING
Raynaud-Spanke 957; Linker 231-1; Mölk-Wolfzettel 400,1 [514]

MANUSCRIPTS
X 190ʳ ♪ (*Robert de rains*), *K* 401 ♪ , *a* (lost, index only)

PREVIOUS EDITIONS
Monmerqué and Michel 1839, 38; Tarbé 1850, 103; Bartsch 1870, 195; Mann 1898, 19; Mann 1899, 97; Aubry 1905, 16 ♪ , XIV ♪ ; Riemann 1905, 837 ♪ ; Lachèvre and Guégan 1914, 9ʳ; Lachèvre et al. 1917, 32, 54 ♪ (French translation); Gennrich 1951, 37 ♪ ; Gennrich 1954, 2:28 ♪ ; Gennrich 1955–56, 2:24 ♪ ; Toja 1976, 456; Tischler 1997, 7: no. 567 ♪

VERSIFICATION AND MUSICO-POETIC FORM
3, *coblas singulars* in *oda continua*; *rime en écho* (1–3), *rime léonine* (1–3), *rime paronyme* (1–3), *rime riche* (1–3)

	1	2	3	4	5	6	7	8	9	10	11	12	13
	7a′	1a′	5b	2b	7a′	1a′	5c	3c	7b	2b	5d	3d	7b

	1	2	3
a′	estre	ele	oie
b	ot	ant/ent	ust
c	ant	ier	ez
d	ont	or	ieus

1.1 Touse] Bergier *(reading from a)* — 2.9 Ot son] son douz *(em. Bartsch)* — 2.10 En alant *(+1) (em. Bartsch)* — 2.13 Entracoler *(em. Bartsch)* — 3.5 a mengier] mengie *(reading from K)* — 3.7 pevres *(reading from K)* — 3.11 formentiex

TEXTUAL VARIANTS
1.1 Bergier *K* — 1.13 d'un] du *K* — 2.9 son douz cuer *K* — 2.10 En alant *K* — 2.13 Entracoler et besant *K* — 3.13 la bele] ma dame *K*

NOTES TO THE MUSICAL TRANSCRIPTION
I, II, V *tractus* on both sides of last two pitches added — III, VII *tractus* added after last pitch — IV last two pitches on "enblant" notated a second higher: emended as in *K* — IV, VI *tractus* on both sides of last three pitches added

MUSICAL VARIANTS
I a' ("-se") *K*

COMMENTARY
This piece deploys intensive echoing, a stylistic hallmark of Robert de Reims's poetry (see also 4a, 4b, and Introduction). The pattern of echoing touches on music as well as text, since the echo rhymes at the end of phrases I, III, IV, and VI reiterate the musical sonorities. In order to make this compositional feature obvious in the musical edition, we present the echoing phrases right after the echoed ones, rather than grant them their own lines. — 1.1, I The incipit *Touse de vile campestre* appears in manuscript *a*, fol. 3ʳ, as the first item under the rubric "Ce sont pastoureles," indexed to fol. 124 (in the contemporaneous foliation); this folio is missing. At the bottom of the right-hand column of fol. 123ᵛ (fol. 108ᵛ in the modern pagination), there is a note in an unidentified early modern hand (Tyssens 1998, 33) that points to the lacuna between fols. 108ᵛ and 109ʳ, with specific mention of the incipit of this pastourelle.

Quant fueillissent li buison,
Que naist la flor el vert pré,
Que chantent cil oisselon
Contre le tens et la saison d'esté,
Chanter m'estuet par raison,   1.5
Qu'Amors le m'ont dit et comandé,
Qui mon cuer ont detenu en prison
Et grant piece a m'ont afié
De moi rendre guerredon
A ma volenté,   1.10
Et si m'ont doné un don,
Que par droit puis bien chanter:
En non Dieu, je m'en dueil
Et debris pour amer.

Lonc tens servies les ai
D'entier cuer fin et joiant
Et encor les servirai
Por atendre le guerredon plus grant.
Se la bele qui j'aim tant   2.5
De s'amor ne m'aproche autrement,
Mon cuer en cuit retraire sans delai:
En vain ai servi longuement.
N'oncor pas ne m'en repent,
Ne ja ne ferai.   2.10
Se g'ensi n'en puis joïr,
Dire porrai sans mentir:
Et li verz glaiolais
M'a tolu mon ami.

When shrubs leaf out,
when flowers burgeon in the green meadow,
when birds sing
because it's the time and season of summer,
I need to sing for good reason,   1.5
for so I've been told and commanded
by Love, who has imprisoned my heart
and long promised
to reward me
as I wish—   1.10
and has indeed granted me a gift,
for I can [now] rightly sing:
In the name of God, loving leaves me
in grief and torment.

I have long served [Love]
with my whole true and joyful heart,
and will go on doing so
in expectation of the greatest reward.
Unless the beautiful lady I love so much   2.5
responds to me more favorably,
I think I will soon withdraw my heart:
I have long served in vain.
Still, I have no regret,
nor will I ever have.   2.10
If I cannot find pleasure there,
I'll be able to say without lying:
The sprout of green
has taken away my lover.

Quand les buissons se couvrent de feuilles,
que les fleurs apparaissent dans le vert pré,
que les oisillons chantent
au retour de la saison d'été,
il me faut chanter, comme il se doit,   1.5
car Amour me l'a dit et commandé,
[Amour] qui a emprisonné mon cœur
et m'a dès lors promis
de me récompenser
à mon gré;   1.10
et voilà qu'elle m'a accordé un don,
si bien que je peux de plein droit chanter:
Au nom de Dieu, je souffre
et me tourmente parce que j'aime.

J'ai longtemps servi [Amour]
de tout mon cœur fin et joyeux,
et je la servirai encore
dans l'attente de la plus grande récompense.
Si la belle que j'aime tant   2.5
ne se décide à m'accorder son amour,
je devrai retirer mon cœur sans tarder:
j'aurai longtemps servi en vain.
Mais je n'ai aucun regret
et n'en aurai jamais.   2.10
Ainsi, si je ne puis jouir de [cet amour],
je pourrai dire sans mentir:
Et le vert glaïeul
m'a enlevé mon ami.

I
Quant fueil - lis - sent li bui - son,
Lonc tens ser - vi - es les ai

II
Que naist la flor el vert pré,
D'en - tier cuer fin et joi - ant

III
Que chan - tent cil ois - se - lon
Et en - cor les ser - vi - rai

IV
Con - tre le tens et la sai - son d'es - té,
Por a - ten - dre le guer - re - don plus grant.

V
Chan - ter m'es - tuet par rai - son,
Se la be - le qui j'aim tant

VI
Qu'A - mors le m'ont dit et co - man - dé,
De s'a - mor ne m'a - proche au - tre - ment,

VII
Qui mon cuer ont de - te - nu en pri - son
Mon cuer en cuit re - trai - re sans de - lai:

VIII
Et grant piece a m'ont a - fi - é
En vain ai ser - vi lon - gue - ment.

IX
De moi ren - dre guer - re - don
N'on - cor pas ne m'en re - pent,

X
A ma vo - len - té,
Ne ja ne fe - rai.

XI
Et si m'ont do - né un don,
Se g'en - si n'en puis jo - ir,

XII
Que par droit puis bien chan - ter:
Di - re por - rai sans men - tir:

XIII
En non Dieu, je m'en dueil
Et li verz gla - io - lais

XIV
Et de - bris pour a - mer.
M'a to - lu mon a - mi.

CATALOGUING
Raynaud-Spanke 1852; Linker 231-7; Mölk-Wolfzettel 714,1 [789]; van den Boogaard
670/1242

MANUSCRIPTS
X 190^{r–v} ♫ (*Robert de rains*)

PREVIOUS EDITIONS

Simonds 1895, 339; Mann 1898, 22; Mann 1899, 100; Lachèvre and Guégan 1914, 10ʳ; Lachèvre et al. 1917, 32, 55 ♫ (French translation); Gennrich 1926–27, 35 ♫ ; Tischler 1982, 2:1573 ♫ ; Tischler 1997, 12: no. 1062 ♫

VERSIFICATION AND MUSICO-POETIC FORM

2, *coblas singulars* in *oda continua*; *rime dérivée* (1), *rime léonine* (1–2), *rime riche* (1–2)

	1	2	3	4	5	6	7	8	9	10	11	12	13	14
1	7a	7b	7a	10b	7a	9b	10a	8b	7a	5b	7a	7c	*6x*	*6c*
2	7a	7b	7a	10b	7b	9b	10a	8b	7b	5a	7c	7c	*6a**	*6c•*

	1	2
a	on	ai
b	é	ant/ent
c	er	ir
a*		ais
c•		i
x	ueil	

REFRAINS

1.13–14 vdB 670 (without concordance) — 2.13–14 vdB 1242 (without concordance)

REJECTED TEXTUAL READINGS

See motet version (7b)

1.9 moi] mon *(reading from Mo)* — 1.14 damer *(–1) (reading from Mo)* — 2.7 en cuit] ensint *(em. Mann)*

TEXTUAL VARIANTS

See motet version (7b)

1.1 florissent *Mo* — 1.12 par moi puisse chanter *Mo* — 1.13 m'en] me *Mo*

NOTES TO THE MUSICAL TRANSCRIPTION

II, VI, XII *tractus* added after last pitch — VIII B♭ signature from "grant" to "-é" — XIV last two syllables are "d'amer" with e′-d′-c′ on "d'a-" and d′ on "-mer": emended after *Mo (see motet version)*; triple *tractus* signaling end of stanza after last pitch and syllable

MUSICAL VARIANTS
See motet version (7b)

COMMENTARY

The motet (7b) clearly predates the song (7a), which is a later adaptation and continuation of it by an anonymous hand. Indeed, the melodic morphology of the motetus is typical of the polyphonic settings on DOMINO QUONIAM, and the second stanza of the song is an exogenous addition that shows versification and poetic quality different from those of the first (see Introduction). — 1.13–14 and 2.13–14, XIII–XIV Several factors allow us to recognize these lines as refrains: their position at the end of the stanza, coupled with divergences in their metrical and rhyme schemes, and a shift in lyric voice. — 2.13–14, XIII–XIV Given the absence of any musical concordance, the refrain of stanza 2 cannot be set to any music with confidence. The fact that the refrains of stanzas 1 and 2 have the same meter allows us to reuse the music of the first refrain for the second, but it should be clear that there is little certainty, in the framework of a *chanson avec des refrains*, that the music of the first refrain was intended for subsequent ones. Note that in this refrain the **a*** rhyme = rhyme **a** plus consonant, the **c**• rhyme = rhyme **c** minus consonant. — 2.13, XIII Literally, "The green gladiolus (or iris)." — 2.14, XIV Note the unexpected masculine *ami* in this refrain-quotation, which suggests a shift to the feminine voice, perhaps beginning at line 2.11, XI.

7b   Quant florissent li buisson / DOMINO QUONIAM   Motet

Motetus
Quant florissent li buisson,
que naist la flor el vert pré,
que chantent cil oiseillon
contre le tans et la seison d'esté,
chanter m'estuet par reison,   5
qu'Amors le m'ont dit et comandé,
qui mon cuer ont detenu en prison
et grant pieça m'ont afié
de moi rendre guerredon
a ma volenté,   10
et si m'ont doné un don,
que par moi puisse chanter:
En non Diu, je me dueil
et debris pour amer.

Tenor
DOMINO QUONIAM

7b   ❧

When shrubs flower,
when flowers burgeon in the green meadow,
when birds sing
because it's the time and season of summer,
I need to sing for good reason,   5
for so I've been told and commanded
by Love, who has imprisoned my heart
and long promised
to reward me
as I wish—   10
and has indeed granted me a gift,
for I, myself, can [now] sing:
In the name of God, loving leaves me
in grief and torment.

Quand les buissons se couvrent de fleurs,
que les fleurs apparaissent dans le vert pré,
que les oisillons chantent
au retour de la saison d'été,
il me faut chanter, comme il se doit,   5
car Amour me l'a dit et commandé,
[Amour] qui a emprisonné mon cœur
et m'a dès lors promis
de me récompenser
à mon gré;   10
et voilà qu'elle m'a accordé un don,
si bien que je peux de plein droit chanter:
Au nom de Dieu, je souffre
et me tourmente parce que j'aime.

Quant flo - ri - sent li buis - son, que naist la flor el vert pré,

Domino [quoniam]

que chan - tent cil oi - seil - lon con - tre le tans et la sei - son d'es - té,

chan - ter m'es - tuet par rei - son, qu'A-mors le m'ont dit et co - man - dé,

qui mon cuer ont de-te-nu en pri-son et grant pie-ça m'ont

a-fi-é de moi ren-dre guer-re-don a ma vo-len-té,

et si m'ont do-né un don, que par moi puis-se chan-ter:

En non Diu, je me dueil et de - bris pour a - mer.

CATALOGUING

Ludwig *Quant florissent li buisson* (137) / DOMINO QUONIAM (M13)

MANUSCRIPTS

Mo 244ᵛ–245ʳ ♫

MATERIAL

Tenor. Melisma from gradual *Hec dies* ℣ *Confitemini domino,* Easter Sunday; biblical reference: Ps. 117:24 ℣ Ps. 117:1

PREVIOUS EDITIONS

Jacobsthal 1880, 280; Raynaud 1881–83, 1:177; Gennrich 1926–27, 35 ♪ ; Rokseth 1935–39, 3: no. 204 ♪ ; Kuhlmann 1938, 2: no. 204 ♪ ; Tischler 1978–85, 3: no. 204 ♪ ; Tischler 1982, 2:1573 ♪

VERSIFICATION

		1	2	3	4	5	6	7	8	9	10	11	12	13	14
		7a	7b	7a	10b	7a	9b	10a	8b	7a	5b	7a	7c	*6x*	*6c*
a	on														
b	é														
c	er														
x	ueil														

REFRAINS

13–14 vdB 670 (without concordance)

REJECTED TEXTUAL READINGS

Motetus. 5 mestuer — 6 m'ont] mon
Tenor. Domino quoniam] Domino

TEXTUAL VARIANTS

See song version (7a)

NOTES TO THE MUSICAL TRANSCRIPTION

Motetus and tenor. Longa before every rest, except motetus at perf. 52
Motetus. Perf. 38 *brevis* on "-re-"

MUSICAL VARIANTS

See song version (7a)

COMMENTARY

See Commentary on 7a

8a Main s'est levee Aëliz   Chanson de rencontre

Main s'est levee Aëliz,
Qui tout son cuer en deliz
A mis et en faire joie.
Seule tint sa voie
Lés un pleseïs.   1.5
La chantoit une mauviz
Qui molt a enviz
A por li ses chans feniz.
Quant ele soz la ramee
Ot haut chanté,   1.10
En une douce pensee
I jut a ma volenté.

Molt ert bele et avenant,
Trop petite ne trop grant.
Face ot blanche enluminee,
Bouche coloree,
Euz verz et rians,   2.5
Gorge blanche come argenz,
[...]
Mameletes ot poignans.
Ileuc s'estoit arestee
Molt porpensans   2.10
De la longue demoree
Que faisoit ses amans.

8a   🖋

Aelis arose early,
her heart all set on pleasure
and having a good time.
She went her way alone,
down toward an enclosed garden.   1.5
There, a thrush was singing;

on seeing her, it most reluctantly
stopped singing.
After [the thrush] on the lower branches
had sung loudly,   1.10
in a gentle swoon
[Aelis] lay there, just as I wished.

She was very pretty and lovely,
not too small, not too tall.
She had a bright face,
rosy lips,
sparkling, smiling eyes,   2.5
a neck as bright as silver,
[...]
Her little breasts were swelling.
There, she had lingered,
deep in thought   2.10
over her lover's
long delay.

8a   ૐ

De bon matin s'est levée Aëlis,
dont le cœur est épris du plaisir
et du divertissement.
Elle s'est dirigée seule
vers un jardin clôturé.   1.5
Là chantait une grive
qui, à son arrivée, a cessé
de chanter, à grand regret.
Lorsque [la grive] sous la ramée
eut chanté à pleine voix,   1.10
[Aëlis], entraînée par une douce pensée,
s'est allongée là, comme je le souhaitais.

Elle était fort belle et charmante,
ni trop petite ni trop grande.
Elle avait le visage diaphane et radieux,
la bouche rosée,
les yeux verts et riants,   2.5
la gorge blanche comme de l'argent,
[...]
Ses seins commençaient à poindre.
Elle s'était attardée là,
fort préoccupée   2.10
par le long retard
de son amant.

I
Main   s'est   le - vee   A - e - liz,
Molt   ert   bele   et   a - ve - nant,

II
Qui   tout   son   cuer   en   de - liz
Trop   pe - ti - te   ne   trop   grant.

III
A   mis   et   en   fai - re   joi - e.
Face   ot   blanche   en - lu - mi - ne - e,

IV
Seu - le   tint   sa   voi - e
Bou - che   co - lo - re - e,

V
Lés   un   ple - se - is.
Euz   verz   et   ri - ans,

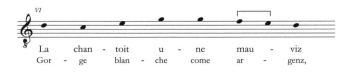

VI

La chan - toit u - ne mau - viz
Gor - ge blan - che come ar - genz,

VII

Qui molt a en - viz
[   ]

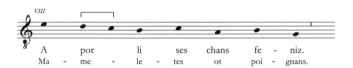

VIII

A por li ses chans fe - niz.
Ma - me - le - tes ot poi - gnans.

IX

Quant e - le soz la ra - me - e
I - leuc s'es - toit a - res - te - e

X

Ot haut chan - té,
Molt por - pen - sans

XI

En u - ne dou - ce pen - se - e
De la lon - gue de - mo - re - e

stanza 1

XII

I jut a ma vo - len - té.

stanza 2

XII

Que fai - soit ses a - mans.

CATALOGUING

Raynaud-Spanke 1510; Linker 231-5; Mölk-Wolfzettel 384,1 [509]; van den Boogaard 689

MANUSCRIPTS

X 190ᵛ–191ʳ ♫ (*Robert de Rains*)

PREVIOUS EDITIONS

Tarbé 1850, 105; Simonds 1895, 338; Mann 1898, 18; Mann 1899, 96; Lachèvre and Guégan 1914, 11ʳ; Lachèvre et al. 1917, 33, 56 ♫ (French translation); Gennrich 1926–27, 34 ♫ ; Tischler 1982, 2:1386 ♫ ; Tischler 1997, 10: no. 862 ♫

VERSIFICATION AND MUSICO-POETIC FORM

2, *coblas singulars* in *oda continua*; *rime batelée* (1), *rime léonine* (1–2), *rime riche* (1)

	1	2	3	4	5	6	7	8	9	10	11	12
1	7a	7a	7b′ (2a+5b′)	5b′	5a	7a	5a	7a	7c′	4c	7c′	7c
2	7a	7a	7b′	5b′	5a	7a	...	7a	7b′	4a	7b′	6a

	1	2
a	iz/is	ant/ans/enz
b′	oie	ee
c(′)	é/ee	

REJECTED TEXTUAL READINGS

See motet version (8b)

1.4 *missing (reading from MüANR)* — 1.5 Lés *missing (–1) (reading from NR)* — 1.9 ele] cele *(reading from MüANR)* — 1.10 Ot] en *(reading from NR)* — 1.12 I jut] muir *(reading from NR)* — 2.10 m. pensans *(–1) (em. Simonds)*

TEXTUAL VARIANTS

See motet version (8b)

1.1–3 *missing in MüA* — 1.5 Lés] uers *MüA* — 1.9 soz] sus *MüA* — 1.10 Ot] a *MüA* — 1.12 I jut] muir *MüA*

NOTES TO THE MUSICAL TRANSCRIPTION

Stanzas 1–2. V, VIII *tractus* added after last pitch — IV this phrase omitted: added as in *NR (see motet version)* with d′ emended to c′ on "voi-", following *MüA (see motet version)* — V note 1 omitted: completed as in *MüA*; b on "un": emended as in *NR* — IX–X these two phrases notated a third higher except pitch on "-me-" notated a fourth higher: emended after *MüANR* — XII triple *tractus* signaling end of stanza after last pitch and syllable —*Stanza 1.* XII ligature bridging d´ and b on "volen-": removed to accommodate the line length, following *NR (see Commentary below)*

MUSICAL VARIANTS
See motet version (8b)

COMMENTARY
The motet (8b) clearly predates the song (8a), which is a later adaptation and continuation of it by an anonymous hand. Indeed, the second stanza of the song is an exogenous addition that shows not only versification and style differing from that of the first, but also a notably unusual thematic treatment of Aelis that contrasts with that of stanza 1 (see Introduction). — 1.3, III Right after "joie," a cross has been traced in lead pencil within the staves, perhaps signaling the omission of the next line and phrase. — 1.9–12, IX–XII The antecedent of the pronoun *ele* is not clear, nor is the subject of the verb *gesir*. — 1.11–12, XI–XII These lines are not given in italics because we do not recognize this refrain (vdB 689), which is as yet only postulated: it has no known concordances, nor does it exhibit any markers suggesting it is a quotation. — 2.11–12, XI–XII In the musical edition, an alternative ending for stanza 2 is necessitated by the fact that stanzas 1 and 2 do not have the same syllable count in line 12: while the music fits the seven-syllable line of stanza 1, a ligature has to be removed to accommodate the six-syllable line of stanza 2.

8b Main s'est levee Aëlis / (MANSUETUDI)NEM   Motet

Motetus
Main s'est levee Aëlis,
ki tout son cuer en delis
a mis   et en faire joie.
Seule tint sa voie
lés un plaisseïs.   5
La cantoit une mauvis
ki molt a envis
a pour li ses chans fenis.
Quant ele sous la ramee
ot haut chanté,   10
en une douce pensee
i jut a ma volenté.

Tenor
(MANSUETUDI)NEM

8b   �explicit mark

Aelis arose early,
her heart all set on pleasure
and having a good time.
She went her way alone,
down toward an enclosed garden.   5
There a thrush was singing;
on seeing her, it most reluctantly
stopped singing.
After [the thrush] on the lower branches
had sung loudly,   10
in a gentle swoon
[Aelis] lay there, just as I wished.

De bon matin s'est levée Aëlis,
dont le cœur est épris du plaisir
et du divertissement.
Elle s'est dirigée seule
vers un jardin clôturé.   5
Là chantait une grive
qui, à son arrivée, a cessé
de chanter, à grand regret.
Lorsque [la grive] sous la ramée
eut chanté à pleine voix,   10
[Aëlis], entraînée par une douce pensée,
s'est allongée là, comme je le souhaitais.

CATALOGUING

Ludwig *Main s'est levee* (252) / ET TENUERUNT (M17), emended to *Main s'est levee* (565a) / (MANSUETUDI)NEM (M71)

MANUSCRIPTS

N 184ᵛ ♩ , *MüA* no. 19, part A, 7ʳ ♩ , *R* 206ʳ ♩ (tenor omitted)

MATERIAL

Tenor. Melisma from gradual *Specie tua* 𝄋 *Propter veritatem*, Common of Virgins; biblical reference: Ps. 44:5 𝄋 Ps. 44:5

PREVIOUS EDITIONS

Bartsch 1870, 210; Raynaud 1881–83, 2:50; Gennrich 1926–27, 34 ♩ ; Dittmer 1959, 165 ♩ ; Tischler 1982, 2:1386 ♩ ; Haub 1986, 142 ♩ ; Saint-Cricq et al. 2017, no. 27 ♩

VERSIFICATION

	1	2	3	4	5	6	7	8	9	10	11	12
	7a	7a	7b′ (2a+5b′)	5b′	5a	7a	5a	7a	7c(′)	4c	7c′	7c
a	is											
b′	oie											
c′	ee											
c	é											

REJECTED TEXTUAL READINGS

Tenor. Nem *missing NR,* Ne *MüA*

TEXTUAL VARIANTS

See song version (8a)

NOTES TO THE MUSICAL TRANSCRIPTION

Motetus. Perf. 2 g′ on "le-" omitted: emended as in *R* (*MüA* missing) — Perf. 8 *tractus* added — Perf. 15 d′ on "voi-": emended as in *MüA* — Perf. 16 c′ on "lés": emended as in *MüA* — Perf. 23 d′ on "ki": emended as in *MüA* — Perf. 25 and 29 *tractus* added as in *MüA* — Perf. 38 note 2 on "pen-" is d′: emended as in *MüA*
Tenor. The untexted melisma [ET TENUERUNT] is erroneously copied in *N.* It is replaced by the tenor melisma in *MüA (see Commentary below)*

MUSICAL VARIANTS

See also song version (8a)

Motetus. Perf. 1–12 lost *MüA* — Perf. 13–26 B♭ signature *MüA* — Perf. 14 e′ ("sa") *MüA* — Perf. 15 d′ ("voi-") *R*; a ("-e") *MüA* — Perf. 16 c′ ("lés") *R*; c′ ("un") *MüA* — Perf. 23 d′ ("ki") *R* — Perf. 26 e′ ("a") c′ ("pour") *MüA* — Perf. 27 b ("ses") *MüA* — Perf. 28 a ("fe-") *MüA* — Perf. 33 g ("ot") *MüA* — Perf. 34 b ("chan-") *MüA* — Perf. 36 c′ ("en") d′-e′ ("une") *MüA* — Perf. 37 f′ ("ne") *MüA* — Perf. 38 f-d′ ("pen-") *R* — Perf. 40–43 "muir a ma volenté" with f′ ("muir") d′ ("a") e′ ("ma") c′ ("vo-") d′-c-′b♭′ ("-len-") c′ ("-té") *MüA*
Tenor. The tenor in *N* is not taken into account *(see Commentary below)*

COMMENTARY

See also Commentary on 8a

In the absence of any mensural source for this motet, the rhythmic mode assigned to the work is based on several clues (ratio of notes between the tenor and the upper parts, placement of grouped notes in the upper parts, *ordo* patterning of the tenor, vertical sonorities expected between parts, distribution of text syllables under the music, etc.).

The scribe of *N* erroneously copied the tenor ET TENUERUNT (M17). The correct tenor melisma is copied in *MüA*, though erroneously identified as NE by the scribe, a syllable usually referring to the last syllable of DOMINE from the gradual *Sederunt principes ℣ Adiuva me Domine* (M3). The scribe's confusion may be explained by the fact that the first five pitches are shared by this tenor and the M3 melisma on NE. The tenor melisma in *MüA* actually matches the syllable NEM of MANSUETUDINEM coming from *Alleluia ℣ Eripe me de inimicis* (M71).

9   Ja mais, por tant con l'ame el cors me bate   Sotte chanson contre Amours

Ja mais, por tant con l'ame el cors me bate,
Ne quier avoir en amor ma pensee,
Quant je voi ce que del tot m'i barate
La rienz el mont que je pluz ai amee.
Encor soit ele pluz gloute que chate,   1.5
Si l'aim je mieuz que feme qui soit nee;
Ne ja ne quit que mon cuer en esbate.

Si con Escos qui porte sa çavate,
De palestiaus sa chape ramendee,
Deschaus, nus piés, affublez d'une nate,
La cercherai par estrange contree;
Soz coverture, ou ait ne clou ne late,   2.5
Ne girrai maiz, tant que j'avrai trovee
Celi por cui j'ai si la color mate.

Merveilles m'ai conment s'est tant tenue
Qu'ele n'a faite aucune forsaillie,
Ou en jardin ou en place ou en rue.
Mais tant connois et son estre et sa vie,
Qu'ele n'iert pas trop longement en mue;   3.5
Ne ja n'iert bien sa terre costoïe,
Tant con el n'ait c'un buef a sa charrue.

Or ai je dit trop grant descovenue.
Ce poise moi, se Dieus me beneïe!
Pluz bele rienz ne fu onques veüe.
Par mal conseill fu la bele ravie;
Més s'ele veut mais devenir ma drue,   4.5
Dont li proi je, ma tres douce anemie,
Ne face mais tel marchié de char crue.

9

Never, as long as a heart beats in my body,
do I care to turn my thoughts to love,
when I see that I am constantly deceived
by the creature I have loved most in the world.
Although she is more gluttonous than a cat,   1.5
I love her more than any other woman alive;
still, I don't think she excites my heart.

Like a Scotsman down at heel,
wearing a patched and tattered cape,
unshod, barefoot, rigged out in rags,
I will search for her in foreign lands;
under no roof of nails and slats   2.5
shall I ever rest, until I have found
the one for whom I have turned so pale.

It's a wonder to me how she has refrained
from cutting any capers
in some garden or public square or street.
But I know her ways and nature all too well:
she won't stay indoors for long;   3.5
nor will her land be well enough tilled
as long as she has only one ox on her plow.

Now I have said something truly improper!
I'm so sorry—God forgive me!
A more beautiful creature has never been seen.
Malign advice took the dear girl away [from me];
but if she ever wants again to be my sweetheart   4.5
(which I ask her, my sweet foe, to be),
let her no longer so easily sell her raw flesh.

Jamais, tant que le cœur battra dans ma poitrine,
je ne désire mettre en amour ma pensée,
quand je vois que sans répit me trompe
la créature que j'ai le plus au monde aimée.
Encore qu'elle soit plus gloutonne que chatte,   1.5
je l'aime mieux que femme qui soit née;
pourtant je ne crois pas que mon cœur s'en réjouisse.

Comme un Écossais qui porte sa savate
et sa chape rapiécée de lambeaux,
sans chausses, nu-pieds, affublé d'une natte,
je la chercherai en pays étranger;
sous un toit ayant clou ou latte   2.5
je ne coucherai que lorsque j'aurai trouvé
celle pour qui j'ai le teint si blafard.

Je m'étonne comment elle a pu se retenir
de faire quelques gambades
dans un jardin, sur quelque place ou dans la rue.
Mais je connais bien sa manière d'être et son genre de vie:
elle ne restera pas longtemps en [sa] cachette;   3.5
et sa terre ne sera pas bien labourée,
tant qu'elle n'aura qu'un seul bœuf à sa charrue.

Je viens de dire une grosse inconvenance:
je le regrette, que Dieu me pardonne!
Plus belle créature ne fut jamais vue;
c'est par mauvais conseil que la belle [me] fut ravie.
Mais si elle veut redevenir ma drue   4.5
(ce dont je la sùpplie), ma très douce ennemie,
qu'elle ne fasse plus tel marché de chair crue!

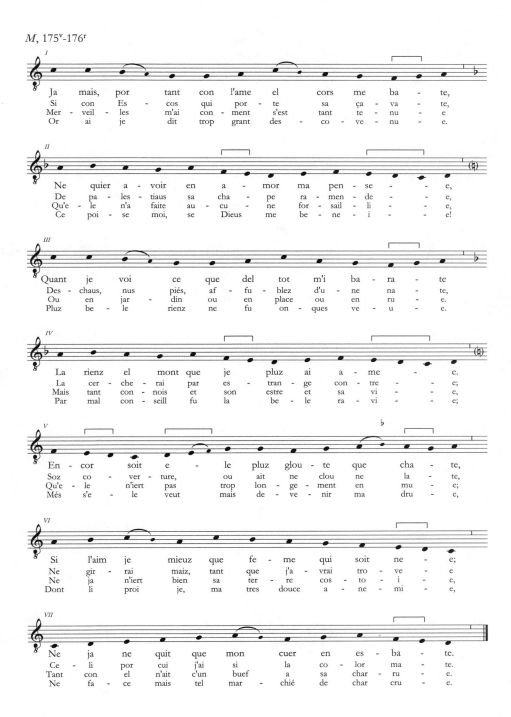

I

Ja — mais, por — tant con l'ame el cors me ba — te,
Si con Es — cos qui por — te sa ça — va — te,
Mer — veil — les m'ai con — ment s'est tant te — nu — e
Or ai je dit trop grant des — co — ve — nu — e.

II

Ne quier a — voir en a — mor ma pen — se — — e,
De pa — les — tiaus sa cha — pe ra — men — de — — e,
Qu'e — le n'a faite au — cu — ne for — sail — li — — e,
Ce poi — se moi, se Dieus me be — ne — i — — e!

III

Quant je voi ce que del tot m'i ba — ra — te
Des — chaus, nus piés, af — fu — blez d'u — ne na — te,
Ou en jar — din ou en place ou en ru — — e.
Pluz be — le rienz ne fu on — ques ve — u — e.

IV

La rienz el mont que je pluz ai a — me — — e.
La cer — che — rai par es — tran — ge con — tre — — e;
Mais tant con — nois et son estre et sa vi — — e,
Par mal con — seill fu la be — le ra — vi — — e;

V

En — cor soit e — le pluz glou — te que cha — te,
Soz co — ver — ture, ou ait ne clou ne la — te,
Qu'e — le n'iert pas trop lon — ge — ment en mu — e;
Més s'e — le veut mais de — ve — nir ma dru — — e,

VI

Si l'aim je mieuz que fe — me qui soit ne — — e;
Ne gir — rai maiz, tant que j'a — vrai tro — ve — e
Ne ja n'iert bien sa ter — re cos — to — i — e,
Dont li proi je, ma tres douce a — ne — mi — — e,

VII

Ne ja ne quit que mon cuer en es — ba — te.
Ce — li por cui j'ai si la co — lor ma — te.
Tant con el n'ait c'un buef a sa char — ru — — e.
Ne fa — ce mais tel mar — chié de char cru — — e.

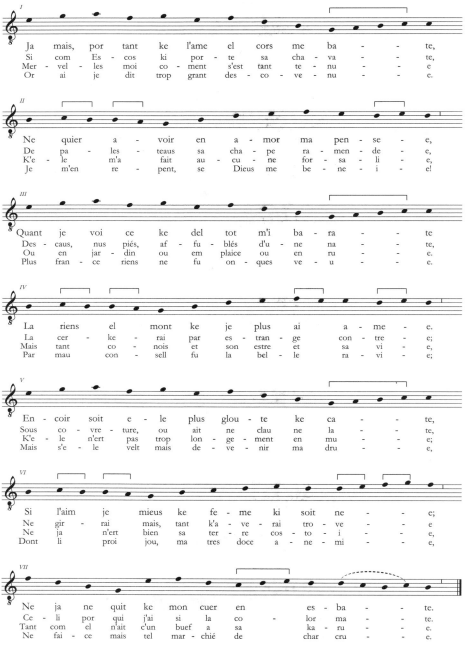

CATALOGUING

Raynaud-Spanke 383; Linker 231-3; Mölk-Wolfzettel 674,10 [703]

MANUSCRIPTS

M 175ᵛ–176ʳ ♪ (*li chievre de rains*), *T* 153ʳ ♪ (*kievre de rains*), *U* 32ʳ⁻ᵛ (empty staves)
(*Le Chievre de Reims*)

PREVIOUS EDITIONS

Tarbé 1850, 66; Paris 1856, 752; Mann 1898, 23; Mann 1899, 101; Lachèvre and Guégan
1914, 11ᵛ; Lachèvre et al. 1917, 33, 57 ♪ (French translation); Mary 1967, 2:6 (French
translation); Toja 1976, 454; Tischler 1997, 3: no. 222 ♪ ; Doss-Quinby et al. 2010, 120;
Tyssens 2015, 1:135

VERSIFICATION AND MUSICO-POETIC FORM

4, *coblas doblas* in *pedes cum cauda*; *rime dérivée* (1), *rime paronyme* (3)

	1	2	3	4	5	6	7
	10a′	10b′	10a′	10b′	10a′	10b′	10a′
	1/2	3/4					
a′	ate	ue					
b′	ee	ie					

REJECTED TEXTUAL READINGS *(M)*

1.5 que] dune *(+1) (reading from U)* — 4.1 descovenue] desconeue *(reading from T)*
— 4.2 Dieus] diex

REJECTED TEXTUAL READINGS *(T, see music)*

1.5 ke] dune *(+1) (reading from U)* — 2.4 La] le *(reading from M)*

TEXTUAL VARIANTS

1.1 con] ke *T*; l'ame] lerbe *U* — 1.2 quier en amor auoir ma *U* — 1.3 ie ce uoi que de
tot me b. *U* — 1.4 je pluz ai] ia plus en *U* — 1.5 Kencor *U*; que] dune *T* — 1.6 mieuz
que feme] plus que nule *U* — 1.7 quier que mes cuers sen *U* — 2.1 Com uns escoz a
son col sa *U* — 2.2 remendeie *U* — 2.4 La] le *T*; Lirai cerchant *U* — 2.5 late] letre *U*
— 2.6 Ne finerai tant que laurai t. *U*; tant kauerai t. *T* — 2.7 j'ai] ia *U*; color] chiere
U — 3.1–4.7 *missing in U* — 3.1 m'ai] moi *T* — 3.2 n'a faite] ma fait *T* — 4.2 Ie men
repenc se *T* — 4.3 bele] france *T*

V "gloute d'une" with g on "glou-", f on "-te", g on "d'u-", and a/b on "-ne" — VII double *tractus* after last pitch signaling end of stanza

V "gloute d'une" with b on "d'u-" and a on "-ne": emended as in the other occurrences of this phrase at I and III — VI, VII *tractus* added after last pitch

COMMENTARY

While the text hand is the same as in the surrounding songs, the music in *M* was clearly entered by a different music hand at a later stage, which probably accounts for the different musical readings in *M* and *T*. The penflourished initial in *M* is also a later addition in a different style than in the surrounding songs. — The attribution in *U* is in the hand of Paulin Paris (Tyssens 2015, 1:135). — 2.1, I According to Paulin Paris (1856, 752), the poet compares himself here to a poor vagabond, wretchedly clothed and shod, for "porter sa çavate [*today* savate]" is evidently an idiom meaning "marcher avec des souliers sans semelle" (to walk in shoes without soles). The image of the Scotsman in the medieval period was unsettled. Recognized for their skill as musicians, the Scots were also repeatedly characterized as "barbaric." In addition, to quote a thirteenth-century proverbial expression, *Li plus truant en Escoce*, "Les plus gueux, les plus demandeurs sont en Écosse" (The most miserable scoundrels and beggars are those found in Scotland; Le Roux de Lincy 1859, 1:285–86). There was also the saying *Larron comme Escossoys* (thievish as a Scotsman; Di Stefano 1991, 284). Guibert de Nogent offers a more favorable picture of the Scots in his account of the First Crusade, *Gesta Dei per Francos* (The Deeds of God through the Franks). What we have in our song is the contrast between a stereotypical Scottish pauper and a man of loving determination.

Works Cited

Anderson, Gordon, and Elizabeth Close, eds. and trans. 1975. *Motets of the Manuscript La Clayette: Paris, Bibliothèque nationale, nouv. acq. f. fr. 13521*. Corpus Mensurabilis Musicæ 68. [Rome]: American Institute of Musicology.

Aubrey, Elizabeth. 2001. "Sources, MS, §III, 4: Secular Monophony, French." In *The New Grove Dictionary of Music and Musicians*, 2nd ed., edited by Stanley Sadie and John Tyrrell, 23:851–60. London: Macmillan.

Aubry, Pierre, ed. 1905. *Les plus anciens monuments de la musique française*. Paris: H. Welter. Reprint, Geneva: Minkoff, 1980.

Bahat, Avner, and Gérard Le Vot, eds. 1996. *L'œuvre lyrique de Blondel de Nesle: Mélodies*. Nouvelle Bibliothèque du Moyen Âge 24. Paris: Honoré Champion.

Bartsch, Karl, ed. 1870. *Altfranzösische Romanzen und Pastourellen / Romances et pastourelles françaises des XIIᵉ et XIIIᵉ siècles*. Leipzig: F. C. W. Vogel. Reprint, Darmstadt: Wissenschaftliche Buchgesellschaft, 1967. Reprint, Geneva: Slatkine, 1973.

Bec, Pierre. 1977–78. *La lyrique française au moyen âge (XIIᵉ–XIIIᵉ siècles): Contribution à une typologie des genres poétiques médiévaux*. Vol. 1, *Études*. Vol. 2, *Textes*. Publications du Centre d'études supérieures de civilisation médiévale de l'Université de Poitiers 6–7. Paris: Picard.

———. 1981. "L'accès au lieu érotique: Motifs et exorde dans la lyrique popularisante, du moyen âge à nos jours." In *Love and Marriage in the Twelfth Century*, edited by Willy Van Hoecke and Andries Welkenhuysen, 250–99. Louvain: Presses universitaires de Louvain.

Beck, Jean. 1927. *Les chansonniers des troubadours et des trouvères, publiés en facsimilé et transcrits en notation moderne*. Vol. 1, *Reproduction phototypique du Chansonnier Cangé, Paris, Bibliothèque Nationale, ms. français no. 846*. Vol. 2, *Transcription des chansons du Chansonnier Cangé, notes et commentaires*. Corpus Cantilenarum Medii Ævi I. Paris: Honoré Champion; Philadelphia: University of Pennsylvania Press. Reprint, New York: Broude Brothers, 1964. Reprint, Geneva: Slatkine, 1976.

———, ed. [1937.] *Anthologie de cent chansons de trouvères et de troubadours des XIIᵉ et XIIIᵉ siècles*. [Philadelphia: University of Pennsylvania Press.]

Bertoni, Giulio. 1917. "La sezione francese del manoscritto provenzale estense." *Archivum Romanicum* 1:307–410.

Boogaard, Nico van den. 1969. *Rondeaux et refrains du XIIᵉ siècle au début du XIVᵉ*. Bibliothèque Française et Romane, ser. D: Initiation, Textes et Documents 3. Paris: Klincksieck.

Bradley, Catherine A. 2018. *Polyphony in Medieval Paris: The Art of Composing with Plainchant*. Cambridge: Cambridge University Press.

Brakelmann, Julius. 1868a. "Die dreiundzwanzig altfranzösischen Chansonniers in Bibliotheken Frankreichs, Englands, Italiens und der Schweiz." *Archiv für das Studium der neueren Sprachen und Literaturen* 42:43–72.

———. 1868b. "Die altfranzösische Liederhandschrift Nro. 389 der Stadtbibliothek zu Bern." *Archiv für das Studium der neueren Sprachen und Literaturen* 42:241–392.

Buridant, Claude. 2000. *Grammaire nouvelle de l'ancien français.* Paris: SEDES.

Butterfield, Ardis. 2003. "*Enté*: A Survey and Reassessment of the Term in Thirteenth- and Fourteenth-Century Music and Poetry." *Early Music History* 22:67–101.

Cremonesi, Carla, ed. 1955. *Lirica francese del medio evo.* Milan: Istituto Editoriale Cisalpino.

Dinaux, Arthur, ed. 1836. *Trouvères, jongleurs et ménestrels du nord de la France et du midi de la Belgique.* Vol. 1, *Les trouvères cambrésiens.* Paris: Tréchener. Reprint, Geneva: Slatkine, 1970.

———. 1839. *Trouvères, jongleurs et ménestrels du nord de la France et du midi de la Belgique.* Vol. 2, *Les trouvères de la Flandre et du Tournaisis.* Paris: Tréchener. Reprint, Geneva: Slatkine, 1969.

———. 1843. *Trouvères, jongleurs et ménestrels du nord de la France et du midi de la Belgique.* Vol. 3, *Les trouvères artésiens.* Paris: Tréchener. Reprint, Geneva: Slatkine, 1969.

———. 1863. *Trouvères, jongleurs et ménestrels du nord de la France et du midi de la Belgique.* Vol. 4, *Les trouvères brabançons, hainuyers, liégeois et namurois.* Paris: Tréchener. Reprint, Geneva: Slatkine, 1969.

Di Stefano, Giuseppe. 1991. *Dictionnaire des locutions en moyen français.* Montreal: Éditions CERES.

Dittmer, Luther, ed. 1959. *Eine zentrale Quelle der Notre-Dame Musik / A Central Source of Notre-Dame Polyphony.* Publications of Mediæval Musical Manuscripts 3. New York: Institute of Mediæval Music.

Doss-Quinby, Eglal, Marie-Geneviève Grossel, and Samuel N. Rosenberg, eds. and trans. 2010. *"Sottes chansons contre Amours": Parodie et burlesque au Moyen Âge.* Essais sur le Moyen Âge 46. Paris: Honoré Champion.

Everist, Mark. 1988. "The Rondeau Motet: Paris and Artois in the Thirteenth Century." *Music and Letters* 69:1–22.

———. 1989. *Polyphonic Music in Thirteenth-Century France: Aspects of Sources and Distribution.* Outstanding Dissertations in Music from British Universities. New York: Garland.

———. 2007. "Motets, French Tenors, and the Polyphonic Chanson ca. 1300." *Journal of Musicology* 24:365–406.

Fauchet, Claude. 1581. *Recueil de l'origine de la langue et poesie françoise, ryme et romans, plus les noms et sommaire des œuvres de CXXVII. poetes François, vivans avant l'an M. CCC.* Paris: Mamert Patisson Imprimeur du Roy. Reprint, Geneva: Slatkine, 1972.

Foulet, Alfred, and Mary Blakely Speer. 1979. *On Editing Old French Texts.* Edward C. Armstrong Monographs on Medieval Literature 1. Lawrence: Regents Press of Kansas.

Gennrich, Friedrich. 1925. "Die altfranzösische Liederhandschrift London, British Museum, Egerton 274." *Zeitschrift für romanische Philologie* 45:402–44.

———. 1926–27. "Trouvèrelieder und Motettenrepertoire." *Zeitschrift für Musikwissenschaft* 9:8–39, 65–85.

———, ed. 1951. *Troubadours, Trouvères, Minne- und Meistergesang*. Cologne: Arno Volk.

———, ed. 1954. *Übertragungsmaterial zur Rhythmik der Ars Antiqua: 101 ausgewählte Beispiele aus dem Bereich der mittelalterlichen Monodie*. 2 vols. Musikwissenschaftliche Studien-Bibliothek 8. Darmstadt: [n.p.].

———, ed. 1955–56. *Altfranzösische Lieder*. 2 vols. Sammlung romanischer Übungstexte 36 and 41. Tübingen: Max Niemeyer.

———. 1957. *Bibliographie der ältesten französischen und lateinischen Motetten*. Summa Musicæ Medii Ævi 2. Darmstadt: [n.p.].

Gérold, Théodore. 1932. *La musique au moyen âge*. Classiques Français du Moyen Âge 73. Paris: Honoré Champion. Reprint, 1983.

———. 1936. *Histoire de la musique des origines à la fin du XIVᵉ siècle*. Paris: Renouard. Reprint, 1971.

Grossel, Marie-Geneviève. 1994. *Le milieu littéraire en Champagne sous les Thibaudiens (1200–1270)*. 2 vols. Orléans: Paradigme.

Haines, John. 1998. "The Musicography of the 'Manuscrit du Roi.'" PhD diss., University of Toronto.

Haub, Rita, ed. 1986. *Die Motetten in der Notre-Dame-Handschrift Mü A (Bayer. Staatsbibl., Cod. gall. 42)*. Münchner Editionen zur Musikgeschichte 8. Tutzing: Hans Schneider.

Hofmann, K. 1867. "Eine Anzahl altfranzösischer lyrischer Gedichte aus dem Berner Codex 389." *Sitzungsberichte der königl. bayer. Akademie der Wissenschaften zu München* 2:486–527.

Hunt, Tony, ed. 2006. *Les Cantiques Salemon: The Song of Songs in MS Paris BNF fr. 14966*. Medieval Women: Texts and Contexts 16. Turnhout: Brepols.

Huot, Sylvia. 1987. *From Song to Book: The Poetics of Writing in Old French Lyric and Lyrical Narrative Poetry*. Ithaca: Cornell University Press.

———. 1997. *Allegorical Play in the Old French Motet: The Sacred and the Profane in Thirteenth-Century Polyphony*. Stanford: Stanford University Press.

Jacobsthal, Gustav. 1880. "Die Texte der Liederhandschrift von Montpellier H. 196." *Zeitschrift für romanische Philologie* 4:35–64, 278–317.

Jeanroy, Alfred. 1899. Review of Mann 1898. *Romania* 28:456–57.

———. 1918. *Bibliographie sommaire des chansonniers français du moyen âge*. Classiques Français du Moyen Âge 18. Paris: Honoré Champion. Reprint, 1965.

Jeanroy, Alfred, and Arthur Långfors, eds. 1921. *Chansons satiriques et bachiques du XIIIᵉ siècle*. Classiques Français du Moyen Âge 23. Paris: Honoré Champion. Reprint, Geneva: Slatkine, 1974.

Juvigny, Rigoley de, ed. 1772–73. *Les bibliothéques françoises de La Croix du Maine et de Du Verdier*. 6 vols. Paris: Michel Lambert.

Karp, Theodore. 1964. "The Trouvère MS Tradition." In *The Department of Music, Queens College of the City University of New York: Twenty-Fifth Anniversary Festschrift (1937–1962)*, edited by Albert Mell, 25–52. New York: Queens College of the City University of New York.

Kuhlmann, Georg. 1938. *Die zweistimmigen französischen Motetten des Kodex Montpellier, Faculté de Médecine H 196 in ihrer Bedeutung für die Musikgeschichte des 13. Jahrhunderts*. 2 vols. Würzburg: Konrad Triltsch.

Lachèvre, Frédéric, and Bertrand Guégan, eds. 1914. *Les chansons de Robert la Chievre de Reims, trouvère du XIIIe siècle*. Paris: Lahure.

Lachèvre, Frédéric, Madeleine Lachèvre, and [Émile-Jules] Grillot de Givry, eds. 1917. *Les chansons de Robert la Chièvre de Reims, trouvère du XIIIe siècle*. Morlaix: Alfred Lajat.

Leach, Elizabeth Eva. 2018. "The Genre(s) of Medieval Motets." In *A Critical Companion to Medieval Motets*, edited by Jared Hartt, 15–41. Woodbridge: Boydell Press.

Lepage, Yvan, ed. 1994. *L'œuvre lyrique de Blondel de Nesle*. Nouvelle Bibliothèque du Moyen Âge 22. Paris: Honoré Champion.

———. 2001. *Guide de l'édition de textes en ancien français*. Paris: Honoré Champion.

Le Roux de Lincy, Antoine Jean Victor, ed. 1841–42. *Recueil de chants historiques français, depuis le XIIe jusqu'au XVIIIe siècle*. 2 vols. Paris: Charles Gosselin. Reprint, Geneva: Slatkine, 1969.

———. 1859. *Le livre des proverbes français, précédé de recherches historiques sur les proverbes français et leur emploi dans la littérature du moyen âge et de la renaissance*. 2nd ed. 2 vols. Paris: Adolphe Delahays. Reprint, Geneva: Slatkine, 1968.

Linker, Robert White. 1979. *A Bibliography of Old French Lyrics*. University, Miss.: Romance Monographs.

Ludwig, Friedrich. 1910. *Repertorium organorum recentioris et motetorum vetustissimi stili*. 2 vols. Halle: Max Niemeyer. Revised by Luther Dittmer. 2 vols. in 3. Musicological Studies 7, 17, and 26. New York: Institute of Mediæval Music; Hildesheim: Georg Olms, 1964–78.

Lug, Robert. 2000. "Katharer und Waldenser in Metz: Zur Herkunft der ältesten Sammlung von Trobador-Liedern (1231)." In *Okzitanistik, Altokzitanistik und Provenzalistik: Geschichte und Auftrag einer europäischen Philologie*, edited by Angelica Rieger, 249–74. Frankfurt am Main: Peter Lang.

———. 2012. "Politique et littérature à Metz autour de la *Guerre des Amis* (1231–1234): Le témoignage du Chansonnier de Saint-Germain-des-Prés." In *Lettres, musique et société en Lorraine médiévale: Autour du* Tournoi de Chauvency *(Ms. Oxford Bodleian Douce 308)*, edited by Mireille Chazan and Nancy Freeman Regalado, 451–86. Publications Romanes et Françaises 255. Geneva: Droz.

Mann, Wilhelm, ed. 1898. *Die Lieder des Dichters Robert de Rains, genannt La Chievre*. Halle: Druck von Ehrhardt Karras.

———, ed. 1899. "Die Lieder des Dichters Robert de Rains, genannt La Chievre." *Zeitschrift für romanische Philologie* 23:79–116.

Mary, André, ed. 1967. *Anthologie poétique française: Moyen Âge*. 2 vols. Paris: Garnier-Flammarion.

Mölk, Ulrich, and Friedrich Wolfzettel. 1972. *Répertoire métrique de la poésie lyrique française des origines à 1350*. Munich: Wilhelm Fink.

Monmerqué, Louis Jean Nicolas, and Francisque Michel, eds. 1839. *Théâtre français au moyen-age [sic] (XIe–XIVe siècles), publié d'après les manuscrits de la Bibliothèque du roi*. Paris: H. Delloye.

Paden, William, ed. and trans. 1987. *The Medieval Pastourelle*. 2 vols. Garland Library of Medieval Literature A, 34–35. New York: Garland.

Paris, Paulin. 1856. "Chansonniers des trouvères." In *Histoire littéraire de la France*, vol. 23, *Fin du treizième siècle*, 512–831. Paris: Firmin Didot. Reprint, Nendeln, Liechtenstein: Kraus Reprint, 1971.

Parker, Ian. 1978. "À propos de la tradition manuscrite des chansons de trouvères." *Revue de musicologie* 64:181–202.

Peraino, Judith. 2011. *Giving Voice to Love: Song and Self-Expression from the Troubadours to Guillaume de Machaut*. Oxford: Oxford University Press.

Petersen Dyggve, Holger, ed. 1938. *Moniot d'Arras et Moniot de Paris, trouvères du XIIIᵉ siècle: Édition des chansons et étude historique*. Mémoires de la Société Néo-Philologique de Helsinki (Helsingfors) 13. Helsinki: Société Néo-Philologique.

Raynaud, Gaston, ed. 1881–83. *Recueil de motets français des XIIᵉ et XIIIᵉ siècles*. 2 vols. Bibliothèque Française du Moyen Âge 1–2. Paris: Vieweg. Reprint, Hildesheim: Georg Olms, 1972. Reprint, Geneva: Slatkine, 1974.

Reaney, Gilbert, ed. 1966. *RISM (Répertoire international des sources musicales)*. Ser. B/IV/1: *Manuscripts of Polyphonic Music (11th–Early 14th Century)*. Munich: Henle.

Riemann, Hugo. 1905. "Die Melodik der Minnesänger." *Musikalisches Wochenblatt* 47:837–39.

Roesner, Edward H., ed. 1993. *Les quadrupla et tripla de Paris*. Plainchant edited by Michel Huglo. Le Magnus liber organi de Notre-Dame de Paris 1. Monaco: Éditions de l'Oiseau-Lyre.

Rokseth, Yvonne, ed. 1935–39. *Polyphonies du XIIIᵉ siècle: Le manuscrit H 196 de la Faculté de Médecine de Montpellier*. 4 vols. Paris: Éditions de l'Oiseau-Lyre.

Rosenberg, Samuel N., with Eglal Doss-Quinby. 2016 [2018]. "Philological Complement to *Motets from the Chansonnier de Noailles* (BnF f. fr. 12615), Part 1: Language of the Scribe and Versification." *Textual Cultures* 10.2:51–75.

Rosenberg, Samuel N., Margaret Switten, and Gérard Le Vot, eds. and trans. 1998. *Songs of the Troubadours and Trouvères: An Anthology of Poems and Melodies*. Garland Reference Library of the Humanities 1740. New York: Garland.

Saint-Cricq, Gaël. 2013. "A New Link Between the Motet and Trouvère Chanson: The *pedes-cum-cauda* Motet." *Early Music History* 32:179–223.

———. 2018. "Motets in Chansonniers and the Other Culture of the French Thirteenth-Century Motet." In *A Critical Companion to Medieval Motets*, edited by Jared Hartt, 225–42. Woodbridge: Boydell Press.

———. 2019. "Genre, Attribution and Authorship: Robert de Reims vs 'Robert de Rains.'" Old French texts and English translations by Eglal Doss-Quinby and Samuel N. Rosenberg. *Early Music History* 38:141–213.

Saint-Cricq, Gaël, with Eglal Doss-Quinby and Samuel N. Rosenberg, eds. and trans. 2017. *Motets from the Chansonnier de Noailles*. Recent Researches in the Music of the Middle Ages and Early Renaissance 42. Middleton, Wisc.: A-R Editions.

Schwan, Eduard. 1886. *Die altfranzösischen Liederhandschriften, ihr Verhältniss, ihre Entstehung und ihre Bestimmung*. Berlin: Weidmannsche Buchhandlung.

Simonds, A. B. 1895. "Two Unedited Chansons of Robert la Chièvre de Reims." *Modern Language Notes* 10:337–40.

Spanke, Hans. 1955. *G. Raynauds Bibliographie des altfranzösischen Liedes*. Musicologica 1. Leiden: Brill. Reprint, 1980.

Tarbé, Prosper, ed. 1850. *Les chansonniers de Champagne aux XIIe et XIIIe siècles*. Collection des Poètes de Champagne Antérieurs au XVIe Siècle 9. Reims: Régnier. Reprint, Geneva: Slatkine, 1980.

———, ed. 1862. *Les œuvres de Blondel de Néele*. Collection des Poètes de Champagne Antérieurs au XVIe Siècle 19. Reims: P. Dubois.

Thomas, Wyndham, ed. 1985–89. *Robin and Marion Motets*. 3 vols. Newton Abbot, Devon: Antico Edition.

Tischler, Hans, ed. 1978–85. *The Montpellier Codex*. 4 vols. Recent Researches in the Music of the Middle Ages and Early Renaissance 2–8. Madison, Wisc.: A-R Editions.

———, ed. 1982. *The Earliest Motets (to circa 1270): A Complete Comparative Edition*. 3 vols. New Haven: Yale University Press.

———, ed. 1985. *The Style and Evolution of the Earliest Motets (to circa 1270)*. 3 vols. Henryville, Ottawa, Binningen: Institute of Mediæval Music.

———, ed. 1997. *Trouvère Lyrics with Melodies: Complete Comparative Edition*. 15 vols. Corpus Mensurabilis Musicæ 107. [n.p.]: American Institute of Musicology; Neuhausen: Hänssler-Verlag.

Toja, Gianluigi, ed. 1976. *Lirica cortese d'oïl*. 2nd ed. Bologna: Pàtron.

Tyssens, Madeleine. 1991. "Les copistes du chansonnier français *U*." In *Lyrique romane médiévale: La tradition des chansonniers. Actes du Colloque de Liège, 1989*, edited by Madeleine Tyssens, 379–97. Bibliothèque de la Faculté de Philosophie et Lettres de l'Université de Liège 258. Liège: Publications de la Faculté de Philosophie et Lettres de l'Université de Liège.

———. 1998. *"Intavulare": Tables de chansonniers romans*. Vol. 2, *Chansonniers français*. Part 1, *a (B.A.V., Reg. lat. 1490), b (B.A.V., Reg. lat. 1522), A (Arras, Bibliothèque Municipale 657)*. Studi e Testi 388. Vatican City: Biblioteca Apostolica Vaticana.

———, ed. 2015. *Le chansonnier français U, publié d'après le manuscrit Paris, BNF, fr. 20050*. Vol. 1. Publications de la Société des anciens textes français. Abbeville: F. Paillart for the Société des anciens textes français.

Van der Werf, Hendrik. 1989. *Integrated Directory of Organa, Clausulæ, and Motets of the Thirteenth Century*. Rochester: Published by the author.

Wackernagel, Wilhelm, ed. 1846. *Altfranzösische Lieder und Leiche aus Handschriften zu Bern und Neuenburg*. Basel: Schweighauserische Buchhandlung.

Index of First Lines